ULTIMATE GUIDE
to SCRAPBOOKING

EVERYTHING You Need to Know From the Editors of Memory Makers

MEMORY
MAKERS
BOOKS

P9-DDB-334

Managing Editor MaryJo Regier
Art Director Nick Nyffeler
Book Editors Amy Glander, Emily Curry Hitchingham, Jodi Amidei
Magazine Editors Darlene D'Agostino, Kari Hansen, Sarah Kelly, Trish McCarty-Luedke, Deborah Mock
Designers Jordan Kinney, Robin Rozum
Art Acquisitions Editor Janetta Abucejo Wieneke
Craft Editor Jodi Amidei
Photographer Ken Trujillo
Writer Lydia Rueger
Editorial Support Karen Cain, Dena Twinem
Contributing Memory Makers Masters Jennifer Bourgeault, Jenn Brookover, Susan Cyrus, Lisa Dixon, Brandi Ginn, Angie Head, Jodi Heinen,
Kelli Noto, Heidi Schueller, Torrey Scott, Trudy Sigurdson, Andrea Lyn Vetten-Marley, Samantha Walker, Sharon Whitehead

Memory Makers® Ultimate Guide to Scrapbooking

Published by Memory Makers Books, an imprint of F+W Publications, Inc.
12365 Huron Street, Suite 500, Denver, CO 80234
Phone 1-800-254-9124

First edition. Manufactured in China.

09 08 07 06 05   5 4 3 2 1

Library of Congress-in-Publication Data

Ultimate guide to scrapbooking : everything you need to know from the editors of Memory
Makers.-- 1st ed.
   p. cm.
   Includes index.
   ISBN 1-892127-65-2
   1. Photograph albums. 2. Scrapbooks--Equipment and supplies. I. Memory Makers
Books.

TR465.U48 2005
745.593--dc22

2005052265

Distributed to trade and art markets by
F+W Publications, Inc.
4700 East Galbraith Road, Cincinnati, OH 45236
Phone (800) 289-0963
ISBN 1-892127-65-2

Distributed in Canada by Fraser Direct
100 Armstrong Avenue
Georgetown, ON, Canada L7G 5S4
Tel: (905) 877-4411

Distributed in the U.K. and Europe by David & Charles
Brunel House, Newton Abbot, Devon, TQ12 4PU, England
Tel: (+44) 1626 323200, Fax: (+44) 1626 323319
E-mail: mail@davidandcharles.co.uk

Distributed in Australia by Capricorn Link
P.O. Box 704, S. Windsor NSW, 2756 Australia
Tel: (02) 4577-3555

Memory Makers Books is the home of *Memory Makers*, the scrapbook magazine dedicated to educating
and inspiring scrapbookers. To subscribe, or for more information, call 1-800-366-6465.
Visit us on the Internet at www.memorymakersmagazine.com.

THIS BOOK BELONGS TO

_____

Dedicated to scrapbookers everywhere who wish to expand their knowledge of the richly rewarding hobby that is scrapbooking.

Emily Curry Hitchingham
Associate Editor, Memory Makers Books

Darlene D'Agostino
Associate Editor, Memory Makers magazine

Amy Glander
Associate Editor, Memory Makers Books

Trisha McCarty-Luedke
Departments Editor, Memory Makers magazine

Jodi Amidei
Craft Editor, Memory Makers Books

Kari Hansen
Craft Editor, Memory Makers magazine

Janetta Abucejo Wieneke
Art Acquisitions Editor, Memory Makers Books

Sarah Kelly
Editorial Assistant, Memory Makers magazine

Lydia Rueger
Former Senior Editor, Memory Makers magazine and Memory Makers Books

Introduction

We are so very fortunate to work in an industry that we are passionate about and even more fortunate to be able to share our valuable and trusted information with you, our scrapbooking audience. In the 8-year history of Memory Makers, it is a rare occasion when *Memory Makers* magazine and Memory Makers Books editors can put their best efforts together in one publication—which is why we're so excited to offer you this book.

Inside the *Ultimate Guide to Scrapbooking*, you'll find everything you need to know about scrapbooking—from the first page to the very last. The book is chock-full of concise scrapbooking solutions and know-how, presented in the user-friendly manner that our readers rely on time and time again.

Each chapter was specially selected for its importance to you, the scrapbooker. From tools and supplies, photography, page design and creative techniques to specialty journaling, computer scrapbooking, maintaining workspace efficiency and cropping on-the-go—we've compiled all of the essential information that no scrapbooker should work without. An illustrated glossary rounds out the knowledge from our arsenal of information to you.

Everything about this book is useful. From its concealed, Wire-O binding that helps it lie flat and its rugged cover, to its convenient carrying size and find-at-a-glance chapter tabs, Memory Makers *Ultimate Guide to Scrapbooking* is perfect for someone new to the hobby of scrapbooking, for on-the-go scrapbookers or for a gift for your special scrapbooking friends. It also makes a great addition to any scrapbooker's resource library.

From our hearts and hands to yours, we hope you enjoy your journey into the richly rewarding world of scrapbooking!

MaryJo Regier
Managing Editor, Memory Makers Books

Debbie Mock
Executive Editor, Memory Makers magazine

Table of Contents

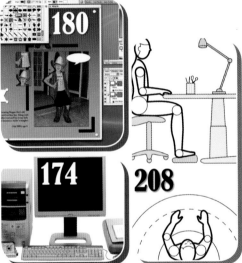

Chapter

Organization and Supplies

Before you start designing scrapbook pages, it's wise to make sure you have the supplies you need and a way to keep them organized. This will allow you to make the most of your time when you sit down to scrapbook. But if you're thinking that organization is the least creative part of this hobby, you might be surprised. With so many great products designed for organization, determining where everything will go and developing systems for keeping an efficient scrapbook arsenal is an art all its own. And many scrapbookers take as much pride in their well-organized home workspaces as their scrapbook pages! With a little preparation, you can too.

Get Organized

It's hard to be inspired by your photos, tools and other scrapbook supplies if you can't locate what you need. Getting and keeping your supplies organized is essential to make the most of your scrapbooking time, and you'll probably uncover useful items you'd forgotten!

ANALYZE HOW YOU SPEND TIME

Keep a time log for a week to identify vacant blocks of time in your schedule for cleaning and organizing your scrapbook space. When are you willing to devote time to getting organized? You may prefer rising 30 minutes earlier each morning or staying up later at night.

Once you have defined the best time to work, identify how you or others may be wasting your precious time and try to avoid those time wasters during your organizational phase. In addition to avoiding time-wasting traps, consider hiring someone else to do housework or baby sitting until you are organized. Don't try to do it all. Use every available resource to squeeze spare moments from each day.

SET SIMPLE, OBTAINABLE GOALS

Start by setting realistic goals for yourself, and determine how often you can devote time to getting organized. Are you realistically able to spend time organizing once a day, week, or month? Make a deadline such as, "Within three months, my workspace will be organized." Once you get there, vow to stay organized.

CHOOSE ONE PROJECT

Looking at "the big picture" can be overwhelming. Select one project with which to begin. Your choices may include setting up your workspace with furniture, lighting and the essentials; sorting years of photos and negatives; or organizing non-consumable or consumable tools and supplies.

BREAK THE PROJECT INTO SMALLER PIECES

Even though you probably understand that the big picture includes organizing your entire scrapbook workspace, it helps to break the task into smaller, more manageable chunks. Isolate one area in which to begin. Collect everything in a large, open space where you can leave things out undisturbed for a couple of days, if necessary.

Finding time to get organized involves making a commitment to the task at hand. Use a calendar to plot out a general time frame in which to get fully organized—even if it is just 30 minutes a day—and try hard to stick with it.

If the process still sounds daunting, rest assured that it can be fun once you begin to see the advantages of getting organized. Get the most out of your time by eliminating distractions. Turn off the phone. Organize in a quiet place out of the runway of the home. By investing time, you will actually be able to gain time to scrapbook. And the sooner you get organized, the more enjoyable and productive your crafting time will become!

Workspace Essentials

Having a space that can be solely dedicated to scrapbooking is ideal for cropping at home. Whether you are setting up a home workspace for the first time or remodeling the space you already have, the following components will help you build a productive cropping environment.

DESKTOP

Tabletop or desk workspace surfaces should measure at least three square feet, but the bigger the better. Store larger tools such as die-cut machines on separate tables to keep your work area clear except for the page you are currently working on. If desired, leave room for a friend to work beside or across from you.

FILING

A file cabinet, a desk drawer, portable accordion file or rolling cart will be necessary for storing all your paperwork: idea sheets, layout sketches, poems and quotes, receipts, etc. Label file folders by topic and store paperwork accordingly.

LIGHT

Good lighting can increase your productivity from 10 to 40 percent and can decrease neck strain, mistakes and headaches. It also allows you to coordinate page elements more accurately. You will need good light not only in the daytime but at night, too. Make sure the lighting you have is clear, natural light (see p. 13). Several light manufacturers make this kind of bulb, which is readily available at hobby and discount stores. Ideally, your work light should come from above your shoulders or from the side onto your work surface.

A productive scrapbook workspace features essential basics like those shown here: Sturdi-Craft modular cabinets, drawer units, pegboard and ample work surface and shelving; Daylight's Scrapbook Lamp™; The Board Dudes' combination cork/magnetic bulletin board; Ergonomic Services' ergonomically correct chair and Rubbermaid's trash can.

POWER

Where are the power outlets? Where is the phone? Orient your workspace around some of these important elements. Cords should not run across walking paths. Generally, it is good to have at least one outlet within five feet of your space. Electricity should be accessible for both accent room lighting and your tools. Easy access to other electronics, such as a computer or radio, is also an important consideration.

SEATING

Most scrapbookers sit while they work, so a quality, comfortable chair is a worthwhile investment. An adjustable chair is best so you can change it to suit your height, thus avoiding neck strain and backache. If your room is carpeted and you want to use a rolling chair, get a plastic floor mat like those used in office settings. "Test drive" a chair in the store before you buy to make sure it works for you.

SHELVING

Every tool and idea book should have its own place, so having enough shelf space is imperative. Shelving comes in all shapes and sizes, from wood bookcases to wire cubes. Make sure you have the size and space you need and that the shelves will bear the weight and suit the dimensions of your intended stock items. Always measure first, then buy or build second.

TRASH CAN

Not only does scrapbooking come with a lot of tools and supplies, it tends to create a lot of refuse. Keep your work area clean by having a trash can or trash bags handy.

VENTILATION

Safety is of primary importance. Proper ventilation and heat are also important aspects to consider. Fumes and excessive heat are not good for you or your photos and paper.

WALL SPACE

Posting notes, ideas and small supplies on a bulletin board or pegboard will keep clutter off your work surface. An area with enough wall space to hang one is ideal.

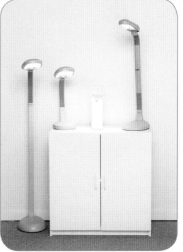

Quality, natural lighting provides true color rendition when matching photo colors to scrapbook supplies. It's also easier on the eyes when scrapbooking for an extended period of time. Some favored scrapbook lamps include (left to right): Verilux's HappyEyes Floor and Desk Lamps, Daylight's Compact Lamp and Ott-Lite Technology's TrueColor FlexArm Plus Lamp. Be sure to check out these manufacturers' Web sites as models and styles differ widely to suit your personal workspace needs.

Archival Issues

Only in recent years have the terms "archival quality," "photo-safe," "lignin- and acid-free," and "buffered paper" become household words for scrapbookers. Today's modern scrapbookers look for products bearing these labels in hopes of creating a safer environment for their photos and albums. As scrapbooking has grown in popularity, more quality supplies and products have become available. Here are some archival terms to know and safety tips to ensure your photos are safe for future generations.

Safer Scrapbooking Products

• *PVC-free plastic page protectors and memorabilia keepers: PVC releases fumes that destroy photos and paper.*

• *Permanent pigment inks: Other inks fade, bleed and spread.*

• *Photo-safe and acid-free adhesives: Other adhesives can damage photos.*

• *Acid- and lignin-free album pages and paper products: Acid and lignin cause photos and paper to degrade and discolor.*

• *Buffered paper: Buffered products help act as a barrier to prevent chemicals from contaminating paper and damaging photos and pages.*

Removing Photos From Magnetic Albums

Remember those old albums with self-adhesive pages and plastic overlays? These albums, sometimes called "magnetic," can cause your photos to discolor, become brittle and deteriorate over time. Here are some suggestions for removing photos from them safely.

- *Slip a slender knife or dental floss beneath a photo's corner to loosen it. Gradually slide the knife or floss behind the photo to remove it.*

- *If photos are firmly stuck to the page, remove them with a commercial adhesive remover such as Big Time Products' un-du PhotoCare™ Solution (shown above). It removes smudges and adhesive residue safely from photos.*

- *If the album's plastic overlay is stuck to your photos, consult a conservator.*

- *Never force a photo from a page. If photos are truly stuck, consider investing in reprints rather than attempting to remove.*

- *Never use heat to loosen photos from a page.*

Photo Organization

All the scrapbook supplies under the sun won't do you any good if your photographs aren't easily accessible. The following storage and organization system will keep the photos you are looking for at your fingertips at all times.

What You'll Need

- *4 x 6" index cards in several colors or photo envelopes*

- *One or more large photo storage boxes*

- *Black journaling pen*

- *Page protectors or a large box if sorting memorabilia (see p. 18) at the same time*

- *Table or floor space that will allow you to leave materials out for a few days*

- *All of your loose photos*

- *Sticky notes for journaling*

- *Any old calendars on which you marked important dates and events*

How To Organize

Gather up all the photos from around the house and bring them into one room. Label an index card for each year of photos that you are sorting. Start sorting your photos into piles by year, placing them near their corresponding index card. Once these piles are made, sort each pile by month or event if necessary. While sorting, jot down memories that certain photos trigger on sticky notes and stick them on the backs of the appropriate photos. If you are unsure when the event in a photo took place, estimate the time frame based on clues in the photo. Ages of children, hairstyles, cars, skirt lengths, hats, shoes and clothing styles all help pinpoint certain eras. File these photos in a separate container to investigate at a later time. Next, slip the photos organized by month or event into archival photo envelopes and place them in a photo storage box. Label the box with a year. If photos from multiple years fit in one box, use index cards to divide by year.

Before you file your organized photos and memorabilia away, be sure to jot down pertinent information on index cards or sticky notes for future reference when scrapbooking. Label any accompanying memorabilia for future scrapbooking as well.

Storage

How you store your pictures will depend on how often you want to view them, how much work you want to go through to showcase them, and how many of them you have to work with. Do you want all your photos in scrapbooks? Or do you feel the majority can go into sleeve albums or boxes while saving the scrapbooking for the most special photos? Regardless of the storage method you choose, keep in mind that photos are best stored at 60 to 75 degrees Fahrenheit for optimal longevity, away from pipes or possible sources of moisture.

Memorabilia Organization

Photos aren't the only memories worth preserving in albums. You come home from certain special events with ticket stubs, programs, ribbons and other such items. And if you're into family history, chances are you have a few special documents like old telegrams and love letters. Keep memorabilia organized so you don't forget to include it in your scrapbook.

Organization

Sort and organize your memorabilia at the same time you are sorting photos. Organize memorabilia by theme, such as home, military, baby, school, sports, etc., then organize it chronologically. Index what is in each box, page protector or pocket, and label accordingly. It's also a good idea to assign numbers to your boxes or bags of memorabilia that correspond with photos, index cards or notes on the same topic. Make two copies of your index—one for your reference and one to keep in your storage device. For example, glue one listing on the outside the storage box and put the other copy with your organized photos. This will help you locate items quickly when scrapbooking.

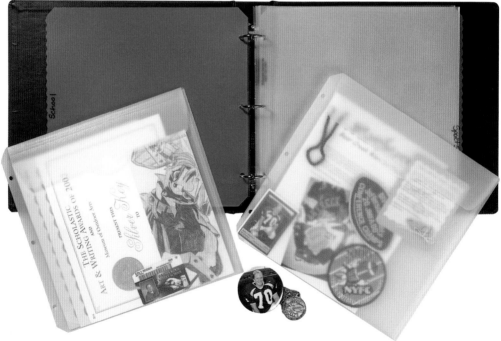

For storing memorabilia in binders, Generations'
Memorabilia Pockets, separated by their Memory Album
Dividers, work well in 12 x 12" binders or albums from
Collected Memories.

For acid-free storage of memorabilia, try (left to right): Highsmith's Acid-Free Memory Boxes, Generations' Memory Express™, General Box Co.'s Tower of Boxes, or for large artwork, maps, etc., try Light Impressions' TrueCore™ Drop-Front Box. Decorate as desired to identify the type of memorabia stored in each box.

Storage

Common cardboard boxes are not a safe solution for document and memorabilia storage, but here are some options that are. Choose what makes the most sense based on the type of memorabilia you have.

BAGS

Polyethylene bags of all sizes are available. There are also specialty zipper-type bags for this purpose that are archivally safe.

BOXES

These are often called rare-book boxes or portfolio boxes. Memorabilia boxes can be purchased at scrapbooking and archival supply outlets. Dry cleaners often have access to acid-free boxes in larger sizes, too. More recently, some scrapbooking vendors have created under-the-bed models from safe plastics, cardboard and other materials.

ACCORDION FILES

Look for acid-free and archival-safe filing systems. Ordinary cardboard office supply styles are generally not archival quality.

HANGING FILES

This is a good option for memorabilia if you have an empty desk drawer. For storing a large quantity of memorabilia along with scrapbook-pages-in-progress, consider Leeco's Cropper Hopper that comes with larger hanging folders.

SCRAPBOOK ALBUMS AND BINDERS

Scrapbooks come in sizes ranging up to 15 x 18" along with archival top-loading page protectors. This size accommodates most larger items and documents. Binders are convenient for adding more page protectors easily (see p. 18).

Non-Consumable Tools and Supplies

Once your workspace and photographs are sorted, you can start focusing on your non-consumable supplies—items that can be used over and over again such as craft knives and paper trimmers. But with reusable supplies comes more maintenance; there is cleaning, repairing, labeling and sometimes discarding, as well as organizing. On the next few pages, you'll learn what to keep in mind regarding all types of non-consumables.

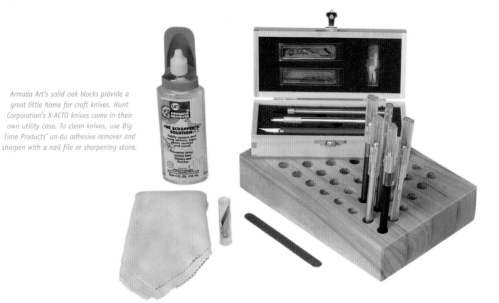

Armada Art's solid oak blocks provide a great little home for craft knives. Hunt Corporation's X-ACTO knives come in their own utility case. To clean knives, use Big Time Products' un-du adhesive remover and sharpen with a nail file or sharpening stone.

Craft Knives

- *Keep them sharp; replace the blades often.*

- *Use an emery board to sharpen larger blades periodically.*

- *Clean blades with rubbing alcohol or un-du adhesive remover to remove any adhesive residue. Dry thoroughly.*

- *Keep the caps on and store out of the reach of children.*

- *Always store your knives in the same easy-access location. This is one sharp tool you don't want to run into accidentally.*

Croppers and Cutters

- *Change the blades of paper trimmers and shape cutters regularly. If you try to save a few pennies on a new blade but end up ruining a photo with a dull cutter, where are the savings?*

- *Clean blades and bodies with alcohol or adhesive remover to remove any residue. Dry thoroughly.*

- *Store out of sight and reach of children.*

- *Store cutters and blades in tightly closed containers for safety.*

Shape cropping tools generally store well in lidded containers, such as this Rubbermaid unit, to keep them dust-free. Frequently used paper trimmers are often most convenient if left on your desktop, so dust occasionally.

Dies and Die-Cut Machines

- Remove any paper bits, particles or dust from dies and machines, using tweezers if needed to get into tiny crevices.

- Organize dies alphabetically or by theme, depending upon the size of your collection.

- Store dies in commercially made wooden-box racks or corrugated storage compartments, specialty binders from the manufacturer or specially made spinning racks.

- Die-cut machines can be bulky and heavy. If you don't use the machine often, store it away from tiny fingers.

Store standard-sized dies in Accu-Cut's laminate towers (available in many sizes), or for smaller dies, try Sizzix/Provo Craft's Die Storage System. Store QuicKutz' dies in the company's EZ-Store Sheets and Storage Binder.

Miscellaneous Tools

Many scrapbook tools have metal and movable parts. Care should be taken to maintain the metal so it remains in prime condition. Because these tools are used quite frequently while scrapbooking, you'll want to keep them handy—preferably on the desktop. Proper care and storage will give you years of use for these kinds of tools: metal straightedge and graphing rulers, hammer, eyelet setter, tweezers, piercing tool, embossing stylus, button-shank remover, round needle-nose pliers and scissors. Keep tools and their handles dry, dust-free and clean of adhesives and colorant residue. Store in a desktop caddy, tool box or in handled totes or zippered bags for cropping on-the-go.

Convenient desktop tool caddies include The Pampered Chef's Tool Turnabout, Westwater Enterprises' Canvas Craft Caddy, Armada Art's Small Art Supply Caddy, Inventor's Studio's Fold 'N Hold' mesh caddy, Twin Ray's Organize-Up clamp-on Craft Space Organizer or ArtBin's Solution Boxes.

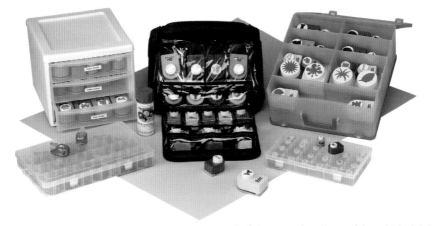

Punch storage comes in a wide array of sizes and styles, including ArtBin's Clear View boxes, Sterilite's drawer towers, McGill's Punch 'N Go tote or Advantus Corporation/Cropper Hopper's Supply Case. Tutto offers a Punch & Stamp Holder carrying tote and Crop In Style provides an over-the-door Punch Pal that can grow with your punch collection.

Punches

- *Remove jammed paper from the punch with tweezers. If that doesn't work, place punch in the freezer for 20 seconds. The metal will contract for easy paper removal.*

- *When dull, punch through heavy-duty aluminum foil.*

- *When a punch sticks, punch through wax paper several times to re-lubricate.*

- *Use adhesive remover to clean off residue left by stickers, tape and self-adhesive paper. Simply squirt the solution on the underside of the punch. Punch through scrap paper until all of the solvent has evaporated.*

- *Keep track of which punches you own. Punch samples of each one from black paper and mount on white cardstock. Label each with name, size and brand. Add this reference to a scrapbook inventory notebook.*

- *Store in over-the-door pocket organizers, bins, toolboxes or plastic drawer units (shown above). These clear cases will protect your punches from dust and moisture while keeping them visible. For cropping on-the-go, take punches in special totes, bags and carryalls made specifically for this purpose.*

- *Temperatures below 32 degrees Fahrenheit may be harmful to the plastic casings. Repeated cold temperatures make plastics brittle before their time. Try not to let your punches freeze. Do not leave them in the car overnight if you live in a cold climate.*

Scissors

- Clean all metal blades, both regular and decorative, with adhesive remover after cutting through adhesive-backed papers.

- Decorative scissors are hard to sharpen professionally. Cut through heavy-duty aluminum foil or soft grade sandpaper to bring back their edge.

- Straightedge scissors can be sharpened professionally at any hardware or fabric store. Or you can do it yourself with a sharpening stone. Hand-held stones are often sold in the scissor section of fabric stores.

Scissor storing solutions include Plaid's Creative Gear scissor holder tote, Crop In Style's tri-fold Scissor Caddy and Armada Arts' solid oak stand.

Stamps

- Clean rubber stamps after every use. Use baby wipes, warm soapy water or commercial stamp cleaner with a sponge or flat stamp scrubber. Use a toothbrush to remove the ink from finely detailed designs.

- Dry completely with a lint-free cloth to avoid mildew on the rubber. Blot stamps gently on towel instead of rubbing them.

- If you have a large stamp collection, sort stamps by design theme, style, artist, brand or alphabetically.

- Keep an inventory of all the stamps you own for quick identification and to avoid duplicate purchases. Stamp each image on paper in a notebook, sorted in one of the categories above.

- Store stamps in stamp travel cases or totes or in commercially manufactured stamp storage units made of wood or corrugated cardboard.

- Store rubber-side-down so you can see the image on the handle. Do not stack rubber stamps.

- Unmounted stamps can be stored in 3 x 5" or 4 x 6" slip-in-style, photo-sleeve page refills. File these pages by theme or by manufacturer in a three-ring binder. Unmounted stamps can also be stored in CD-ROM jewel cases.

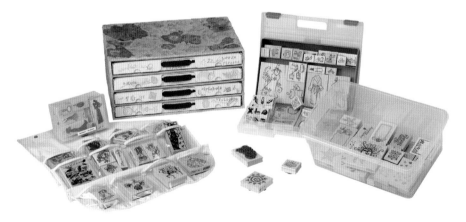

Keep stamps ready for use with Traffic Works' plastic boxes for smaller stamp collections, Highsmith's Stamp Storage Chest & Totes, Eagle Affiliates' Stamp Case, Rubbermaid's wide array of bins or Westwater Enterprises' Craft Pockets.

Consumable Tools and Supplies

Items such as papers, inks, beads, textiles and metallics are great fun in scrapbooking. It's these supplies that give your page added detail and pizazz. But with the glitz also comes guidelines to keep these and other consumable products organized and well cared for in order for you to get the most for your money.

Adhesives

- *Purchase products that are acid-free and photo-safe. Then, organize your adhesives into two categories: wet and dry.*

- *Use a pin or piercing tool to unclog the spouts of bottled adhesives.*

- *Check wet adhesives every two months to see if they are still fluid and usable.*

- *Store tape adhesives on rolls in their original packages when not in use to prevent unraveling or sticking to other items.*

- *Keep tape runner cartridge refills on hand.*

- *A convenient time to remove residue from an adhesive application machine is when you're changing adhesive cartridges. Use adhesive remover and a cotton swab to wipe residue away.*

- *Store all adhesives away from heat sources and out of sunlight.*

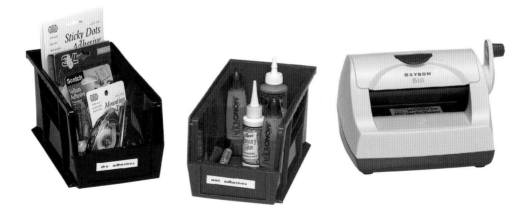

Store sorted adhesives in rapid-access containers such as Rubbermaid's Slim Drawer or Quantum Storage Systems' 4-Drawer Tilt Bin or Stackable or Hangable bins. Keep your Xyron machine clean by removing any sticky residue with an adhesive remover.

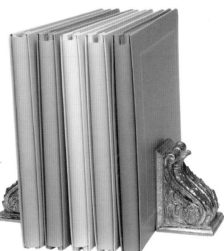

Store albums, such as these from Colorbök, upright on open shelving or in bookcases that are deep enough to accommodate the albums' widths. Avoid packing albums tightly together; excessive compression can damage pages over time.

Albums

- Select albums that are acid- and lignin-free, with page protectors made of polypropylene or polyethylene plastics.

- Consider the album's spine for longevity. For example, steel closures always last longer than simple adhesive or sewn fiber bindings.

- Albums are available in a number of sizes. Shelves or bookcases should be deep enough so that the albums do not hang over the edge. This avoids needless bumping and tipping.

- Store upright on a shelf, leaving a tiny bit of "breathing room" between albums. Excessive compression could damage photos over time and crush page accents.

- Use a clear dust jacket to protect the album's cover from hand oils, dust and pollutants.

- If storing albums on open shelving, avoid sunlight and keep albums as dust-free as possible. Large computer monitor dust covers, available at office supply stores, can cover multiple albums.

- Spines should be labeled when possible and face outward so you can read them.

- Avoid the use of magnetic photo albums with static, liftable sleeves. They may be labeled "archival," yet these have been known to be hazardous to photos.

Cleaners and Fixatives

- *If possible, keep cleaners, fixatives, solvents and sprays in a locked toolbox if there are small children in the house.*

- *Keep caps on tightly when products are not in use. Some cleaners evaporate rapidly and fumes can be overwhelming.*

- *Do not mix chemicals. Allow time for complete drying between chemical processes such as spraying with an archival fixative, using adhesive remover or inks, heat embossing, or applying liquid lacquers.*

- *Be careful when using these products near a heat embossing gun. Flammable products should not be used in the same room as one. Read all label cautions when using these products indoors.*

If possible, keep cleaners in a locked toolbox for safety's sake. Read all label cautions so you know what you are working with.

Try Paintier Products' Paintier 40 Carousel for storing enamels, lacquers and paints.

Colorants

The selection of colorants for scrapbookers has expanded beyond basic pens, markers and ink pads to include chalks, paints and pigment powders, to name a few. Each colorant has its own distinct characteristics and unique properties, which impacts its own care and organization needs. These ideas should help you tame your coloring tools and supplies.

Lacquers, Paints, Powders and More

- *Keep watercolor paint palettes in good condition by mixing different paints on an old CD rather than on the paint palette.*

- *Do not mix pearl pigment powders and water in the original containers. You are not likely to use all of the colorant in one sitting and would end up wasting it.*

- *Store acrylic and stencil paints right-side up. Use within a year.*

- *Keep paintbrushes clean and store carefully to prevent damage to brush tips.*

- *If you use sponges to apply paint, be sure to wash them out with warm, soapy water and let dry for 48 hours before storing in a closed container.*

- *Close clear lacquers tightly after use. Even a little air flow will dry the liquid. Use a sewing needle to unclog the lid dispensers of lacquer bottles.*

- *Test lacquer to see if it is dry (firm) after 24 hours before adhering the lacquered element to a scrapbook page.*

- *Organize paints and powders by grouping together by brand, type or color.*

Embossing Powders

- *Embossing powders, used primarily with stamping inks, come in many colors and textures, such as extra thick, fine, pearl, tinsel and foil. Organize embossing powders by type or color.*

- *Seal tightly after use. Powder is loose and can make a mess.*

- *When sprinkling powders onto stamped images, work over a sheet of paper or a plastic tray with a spout specially designed for stamping. Then, pour excess powder back into jar to avoid waste.*

- *Beware of the fumes. When heated, embossing powders release fumes as they turn from a solid to a liquid state. Do not inhale fumes and work in a well-ventilated area.*

- *Store powders away from heat, moisture and water.*

- *Store in original jars on spinning racks, in trays, in stamp caddies, in bins or drawers. Storing powders upside down will enable you to see the powder colors easier.*

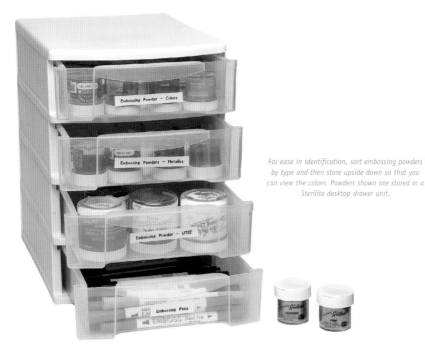

For ease in identification, sort embossing powders by type and then store upside down so that you can view the colors. Powders shown are stored in a Sterilite desktop drawer unit.

Pens and Markers

- Use high-quality pens for scrapbook journaling. Look for acid-free, fade- and waterproof pigment ink.

- Don't lose the caps. The minute you open a pen, you are in a race against evaporation.

- Use your pens at least once a week if possible. This keeps the ink flowing and the tips mobile.

- Many pens are not safe for writing on photo backs. If you want to write on your photos, do so in an inconspicuous place such as a corner. Better yet, use a soft pencil meant for writing on the backs of photos.

- If you use a spray bulb to splatter ink from pen tips onto your scrapbook pages, immediately wipe the bulb tip with a damp cloth after each use to keep the tip color-free.

- Sort your pens regularly and toss out those that have dried out.

- Sort your pens by color, by type or brand. Various types of pen points include calligraphy, brush, writer, scroll, bullet and chisel.

- Keep an inventory of what pens, tips, brands and colors you own to prevent duplication.

- While pen manufacturers' opinions vary about whether horizontal or vertical storage is best for pens, we recommend you store pens horizontally at least 90 percent of the time.

- Store pens away from heat registers and drafts. Air movement speeds evaporation—even with the caps on.

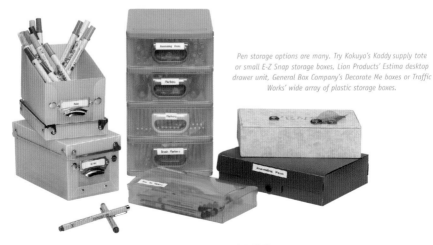

Pen storage options are many. Try Kokuyo's Kaddy supply tote or small E-Z Snap storage boxes, Lion Products' Estima desktop drawer unit, General Box Company's Decorate Me boxes or Traffic Works' wide array of plastic storage boxes.

Chalk

- Keep chalks as dry as possible.

- Avoid dropping chalk cases; chalk palettes are fragile and break easily.

- Clear off extra dust or stray particles after use by blowing gently on your chalks or rubbing the surfaces with cotton swabs.

- When using a chalk palette, do not press or twist your applicator into the chalk. Instead, sweep it lightly across the surface to keep the chalk in good condition.

- Cover your work surface with paper towels before working with chalk.

- Keep a white eraser with your chalk. Chalk mistakes erase easily.

- If you apply chalk with sponge-tip applicators, keep them clean with warm, soapy water. Allow to dry for 48 hours before storing in a closed container.

- Spray chalked artwork with a fixative to prevent chalk particles from scattering.

- Store chalks in their original, compartmentalized containers inside zippered sandwich bags or in small supply cases with or without handles.

Keep chalks and metallic rub-ons in their original palette containers. Store colorant applicators in Provo Craft's Bradletz Drawerz. Larger chalk palettes and rub-ons can be stored in Kokuyo's large E-Z Snap storage boxes. Store Craf-T's chalk enhancers and spray fixatives with cleaners, if possible.

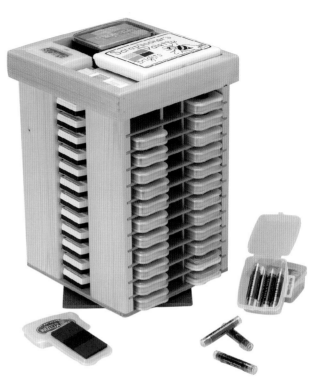

StampPadCaddy.com's Classic Caddy revolving carousel tower keeps ink pads organized and visible, with extra storage at the top for more pads. Tsukineko's ink daubers fit perfectly in TidyCrafts' rectangular Snappy Craft Containers. Other companies that make stamp pad storage include Last Dollar Designs and Port-a-Ink by CDJ Designs, LLC.

Ink Pads & Ink Daubers

- *Make sure the ink you use is safe for your albums. Stamping inks and daubers should be acid-free, fade- and waterproof pigment ink.*

- *Ink pads should be stored horizontally. Some schools of thought believe that ink pads should be stored upside down.*

- *Use ink pads regularly to keep the ink sponges saturated.*

- *Dauber caps tend to fall off easily. Make sure they are secure to prevent dehydration.*

- *Sort and organize ink pads by color, ink types or brand names for easier identification.*

- *Ink refill bottles should be stored upright. Keep the caps on tightly.*

- *Store ink pads in special racks made of wood or corrugated cardboard made specifically for ink storage or in shallow bins, drawers, supply cases or totes.*

Paper

- Keep your paper in a clean, dry place away from direct sunlight to prevent fading.

- Ideal temperatures for paper storage are between 65 and 80 degrees Fahrenheit, with low to moderate humidity.

- To be photo-safe, paper should be pH neutral (acid-free) and lignin-free.

- Many varieties are buffered, which is preferable for scrapbooking projects.

- Pets and small children can cause a lot of turmoil with a paper stack. Keep your paper out of reach of children and family pets.

- Sort and group solid-colored paper and cardstock using the "ROYGBIV" rainbow order. This is red, orange, yellow, green, blue, indigo and violet. Add black, gray, white, cream, brown and tans to the front or the back end of the filing spectrum.

- Sort and group patterned papers by design theme for easier access.

- Not all vellum, mulberry, metallic or handmade papers are archivally safe and thus should not be allowed to directly touch photos and memorabilia on a scrapbook page or be stored with acid-free, archival-safe papers.

(Continued on p. 36)

A great paper storage option is Display Dynamics' flexible, stackable clear plastic paper trays and wood laminate towers. The Paper Station has enough space to hold 30 trays, while the Paper Station Mini can accommodate 10 trays.

Paper, continued...

- If you have a significant collection of vellum, mulberry, metallic or handmade papers, sort by color and/or theme.

- For booklets of paper, you have a number of organization options. You can keep the paper bound in the booklet until ready to use and just organize the booklets on a shelf or binder. Or, tear the patterned sheets from the booklet and incorporate into the rest of your sorted patterned or specialty papers.

- When you identify papers you no longer wish to use for scrapbooking, they can be used for wrapping small gifts, making greeting cards or other craft projects.

- Create a "give-away" folder filled with papers you no longer care for anymore. When the folder is full, donate it to an elementary school, charity or a beginner scrapbooker.

- Store your paper in a manner that makes it easy for you to find it again. Some prefer to sort by manufacturer while others prefer to sort by theme.

- Paper can be stored in a variety of ways. For horizontal storage, store paper flat in corrugated cardboard, wire, wood or acrylic paper racks, trays or shallow drawer units.

- For vertical storage, store paper upright in magazine file boxes, accordion files or hanging files in cropping bins or file drawers. Keep it snugly filed so it does not curl or bend over.

- When storing paper on wire racks, make inexpensive dust covers from bedsheets. Fasten fabric to wire racks with heavy-duty glue dots.

- Secure tall racks to the wall, if possible, to prevent toppling.

- Take a sample sheet of scrapbooking paper along with you when you shop for storage containers. You can test the fit before you buy.

- Keep a 12 x 12" paper keeper in your car for unexpected shopping trips to keep the paper in tip-top shape until you get it home.

Embellishments

The boom in scrapbook embellishments has brought unique beauty and texture to pages along with a storage quandary for the scrapbook workspace. Because these items vary in size and bulk, it can be challenging to arrange them for easy access. How do you sort, organize and store all these baubles and trinkets? Don't fear! Solutions for taming all of your embellishments are right at hand.

To keep tiny metallic embellishments organized, try ScrapKings' aluminum cases with matching tins

Metallics

- *Sort metallics by type—eyelets, bookplates, charms, frames, hinges, nailheads, wire, etc.*

- *Store all metal embellishments in low humidity. Flexible metals have alloys that can rust, as can those containing iron. (Test with a magnet. If a magnet can pick it up, it has iron in it.)*

- *Keep all metals dry and wiped free of hand oils which contain body salts. Salt, water and other chemicals can lead to the corrosion of metal.*

- *Aluminum and copper can oxidize, turning black or green over time, respectively. Make sure these items are not directly touching your photos.*

- *Carry a sample of each eyelet color and size when you shop to prevent buying duplicates. String one example of each color and style onto a large safety pin or a length of wire and tuck it in your handbag.*

- *Store the tiny pieces in containers with compartmentalized spaces such as nut-and-bolt drawers, portable jewelry cases and more. Consider storage that has room for growth.*

Advantus Corporation/Cropper Hopper's Embellishment Organizers provide quick-view access.

Baubles and Beads

- If the baubles are made of glass, stone or fired ceramic, they contain no acid and will not harm photos or scrapbooks.

- Plastic beads and other items are suitable as long as the plastic does not contain PVC.

- Remember that baubles are hard objects that can potentially scratch your photos; don't place photos opposite these items on a facing page.

- To avoid adding excess bulk to a page, use small and flat objects whenever possible.

- Sort such embellishments by size of item and then by color.

- Store in clear containers that permit you to see what's inside and allow you to pour easily into a tray for further sorting.

- Choose compartmentalized storage solutions that suit either your desktop, travel tote or both. Storage systems should allow room to accommodate new items.

Textiles: Fibers, Ribbons, Thread and More

- *Fibers manufactured from natural materials—such as cotton ribbons, threads, hemp, jute and raffia—need to be kept dry for longevity. Moisture invites mildew.*

- *Both natural and synthetic textiles may contain fugitive dyes. Test for color permanence by applying a moist cotton swab to the textile to see if the color spreads onto the swab.*

- *Some fibers last longer if you spray them with archival sprays. These include wood-product fibers, hemp and raffia.*

- *If a textile holds sentimental value, such as a ribbon from a wedding gown or baby boo-ties, it should be encapsulated to protect it from adhesive, light, dust and moisture.*

- *Consider sorting textiles by color family for easier access. For example, keep red fibers, ribbons, embroidery threads and yarn together on the same cardstock "bobbin" or on separate bobbins in the same container.*

- *Try not to bunch textiles; they can wrinkle or become knotted. Winding them around a bobbin or cardstock square is a good option for keeping them straight and tidy.*

- *Floss boxes come with embroidery floss winding cards or bobbins. Wind one fiber type on each card. File these mini cards in the floss box by color. Each box can hold dozens of these small, fiber-wrapped cards. You can also place the bobbins in sticker sleeves and store them in binders.*

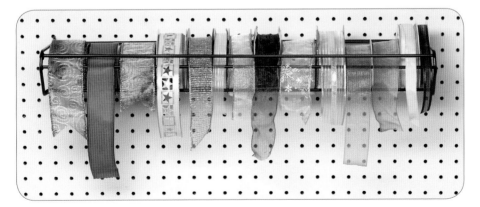

Novelcrafts' sticker dispenser for pegboard pulls double-duty keeping rolls of ribbon organized and ready for use.

Organics: Pressed Flowers, Leaves, Twigs and More

- *Keep all natural materials dry.*

- *Encase flowers and loose petals in vellum envelopes, plastic memorabilia envelopes and pockets or in separate areas where they will not harm photos if they crumble or shed seeds.*

- *Allow flowers to dry at least three months in open air before placing them in a storage container or scrapbook, so that any tiny insect eggs can hatch and leave the organic matter.*

- *Tiny shells, sand or other items that have particles should be encapsulated in memorabilia pockets, plastic envelopes or well-sealed shaker boxes.*

- *Shells should be allowed to dry naturally for two months in open air before you store them in containers or use them in a scrapbook. This allows the body of the animal to decompose inside the shell and not cause odors.*

- *Twigs and bark may cause staining of page elements due to wood tannins. If you use them in scrapbooking, allow them to dry for at least two months. Keep them at least 4" away from photographs.*

- *Whenever possible, keep organic materials flat and stable. Many are delicate and will break if placed in storage containers that are too large, due to excessive movement.*

- *Store organic materials in zippered bags, flat boxes or cases or memorabilia keepers until you are ready to use them.*

For storing organic scrapbooking materials, stick with containers that provide little movement of materials to avoid breakage, such as Akro-Mils' Craft Organizer Caddy.

Kokuyo's Color 'N Color Collection binder with page protectors and an ordinary office binder with page protectors work well as storage options for premade page additions.

Premade/Preprinted Page Additions

- *For scrapbooking efficiency, organize all of your premade page additions by theme—not by type (sticker, punch-out titles, etc.) or by product manufacturer. For example, when you create a winter page layout, you can find all the appropriate accents quickly in the section labeled "winter."*

- *Store page additions flat, either horizontally or vertically. Possible storage containers include accordion-type files, large envelopes, file folders, plastic drawer units, or binders with top-loading page protectors.*

- *Attach die cuts or other page additions onto blank sheets of paper by theme with removable/repositionable adhesive. Store these sheets by theme in page protectors within binders.*

- *Store small sheets of stickers or individual pieces in compartmentalized clear plastic sheets meant for photographs. Store the sheets in 3-ring binders.*

- *Store paper die-cut shapes in boxes, accordion files, hanging files, tilt bins, binders, plastic zippered sandwich bags held on a ring, or inexpensive 4 x 6" photo albums.*

Chapter

Photography

Photographs are the basis for nearly every scrapbook page. In fact, without them, we wouldn't have a hobby called scrapbooking and you wouldn't be reading this book! With that in mind, you'll want the photos on your pages to be the best that they can be, and this chapter can help. Find everything from film speed basics to setting up a photo studio at home and much more. Apply the photo tips and techniques throughout the chapter to create photos that are just as artful as the pages that display them.

Camera Shopping Tips

As a scrapbooker, you want the best possible pictures, so a good a camera is essential. But as a consumer, the hundreds of available models make camera selection downright overwhelming. Setting a budget will help you resist the temptation of unnecessary camera features. You should also beware of the salesperson that tries to convince you that you have to spend more money to get a better camera. There is a great camera for every budget, whether you have $50 or $5,000 to spend.

Photos: Ken Trujillo, Memory Makers

Compact point-and-shoot cameras are similar in size to the many single-use cameras available on the market and all make for quick-and-easy shooting. Choosing the proper film speed in these cameras for shooting indoors or out will provide the best results.

Point-and-Shoot or SLR?

If your budget is not too limited, decide whether you want a new point-and-shoot or an SLR (single-lens-reflex) camera. Point-and-shoots offer built-in features, such as red-eye reduction, automatic flash, macro zoom, self-timers and more. For quick-and-easy photos, a point-and-shoot will suffice. They are great for tossing in your bag and shooting on-the-go.

SLRs offer the ability to experiment with a wide variety of shutter speeds, aperture settings, lenses, filters and more. If you want to learn more about photography or are interested in taking a photography class, an automatic SLR with manual override is a good choice. (Yet another option is a digital camera. Learn more about them on page 175.) Read the owners manual to familiarize yourself with all features, functions and capabilities of a new camera, then shoot some test rolls to ensure all are working properly.

Long the workhorse of many professional photographers, SLR models come in all shapes and sizes. Some SLRs are strictly controlled manually by the photographer while others have fully automatic features with manual-override capabilities. SLR cameras provide the widest range of creative control for photographers.

Film Speed

When purchasing film, you quickly narrow down the brand and number of exposures you want, leaving you with one final choice—the film speed, or ISO number. But what do these numbers really mean?

The number printed on each box indicates how long it takes a 35mm film to react to light when the camera's shutter is open. A smaller number indicates a slower film that takes longer to react to light, while a larger number indicates a faster film that reacts quickly to light.

If you will be taking pictures for different occasions over a period of time, use ISO 200, 400 or 800. These medium-speed films adapt well to a variety of conditions. In bright light, choose a slower film with an ISO of 25, 50 or 100. In dim light where you cannot use a flash, choose 1600 or 3200. When using a flash, use a medium-speed film such as ISO 400.

Keep in mind that while a slower speed film is appropriate for brightly lit conditions, it cannot freeze the action, such as a sporting event. To avoid blurry shots, even in bright light, use ISO 400 or greater. At indoor sports events, where your flash range is often inadequate, use the fastest film you can find so that your camera can stop the action.

Using a zoom lens also affects your ISO selection. When your camera is at its maximum zoom, the shutter must stay open longer, which can cause blurry pictures. You can potentially avoid this problem by using faster films—ISO 400 in daylight or up to 3200 in dim light. When shooting fast action in low light with a zoom lens, using a faster film can significantly improve your results.

In considering the final outcome, slower films (25 to 100) produce the sharpest pictures. For enlargements, use the lowest possible film speed. Prints made from faster films have noticeable grain, especially when blown up.

Photo Duplication

The easiest way to duplicate your photos is by having reprints made from your negatives. But negatives aren't always available, especially with heritage photos. Fortunately, there are ways to duplicate photos without the use of negatives.

TAKE A PICTURE OF A PICTURE

The biggest benefit of this method is that it creates negatives for your photos. A manual 35mm SLR camera—with an inexpensive, close-up or macro lens set—works great for this purpose. Simply place your photo on a flat surface or tape it to a wall in bright, even light, then focus and snap!

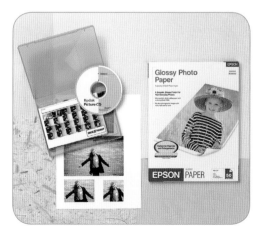

SCANNING PHOTOS/PRINTING DIGITAL IMAGES

To scan your photos at home, use the TIFF file format for high-resolution images. The quality of your duplicated photos will depend on the quality of your scanner, scanning software, printer and the photo paper you print on (shown is Epson's Glossy Photo Paper made specifically for scrapbooking). If do-it-yourself scanning is not for you, you can have high-quality photo scans put on a CD-ROM. To print images from a CD-ROM, a high-quality color printer and photo-quality printer paper will give the best color results. Or, you can get them printed at a photo lab.

COLOR COPY MACHINES

The least expensive duplication option is to use a laser color copier, which is sensitive to the different shades in photographs. Color copiers allow you to change the size of the image.

For preservation purposes, use acid-free, 28-pound or heavier, smooth white paper. Color photocopy toner is known to be more stable than inkjet dyes, so choose color copying over printing with an inkjet printer when possible. Color copy machines can be found at select scrapbook stores or office supply stores.

DIGITAL PHOTO MACHINES

Digital, print-to-print photocopy machines (shown is Kodak's Picture Maker) are user-friendly, self-service machines that can be found at your local discount, photography, drug store or supermarket. Some popular standard features include the ability to make enlargements and reductions, custom cropping, rotating and zooming in, and the ability to sharpen and adjust color and brightness of images. Some allow you to convert a color print to a black-and-white or sepia-toned photo. Many digital photo machines have the ability to print from CD-ROMS or directly from digital camera storage cards.

KODAK Picture CD and KODAK Picture Maker © are registered trademarks of Eastman Kodak Company, 2003. Used with permission.

Photo Restoration

You may have old photographs that are torn, cracked, faded, curled or stuck together. This damage could have occurred in a single instant or gradually over time. The good news is that these photos can usually be repaired. While you might need to call a professional conservator or a photographer who specializes in restoration techniques, there are also steps you can take at home.

BASIC PRECAUTIONS

It's important to know the proper way to handle and work with photographs whether they are damaged or not. Handle photographs while wearing clean white cotton gloves to prevent transferring dirt and oils to images. When possible, store negatives that you might have in archival-quality plastic sleeves in a cool, dry location away from your photos. There is always the chance that photo damage can't completely be undone, and reprinting the photo may be your best option.

ENVIRONMENTAL DAMAGE

Variations in temperature and humidity in basements, attics and garages can cause long-term problems with photos, such as sticking, mold and curling, so proper storage is important. Store photographs in a windowless interior closet in your home away from heat and water sources. Keep your storage area as close to a temperature of 65 to 70 degrees with 30 to 50 percent humidity with as little variation as possible. Store your photos in paper enclosures made of acid- and lignin-free paper rather than plastic.

TORN OR CRACKED PHOTOS

Mishandling or improperly storing photos often results in broken, torn or cracked prints.

Digital photo restoration is a popular option for fixing cracked prints. If you are well-versed in photo-editing software and own a high-quality photo printer, it is possible to scan the picture, repair it yourself and print out a new copy. New developments in scanners and printers are making such projects easier for the common user.

Despite technological advances, if the image is important to your family history, take it to a professional who is experienced in digital photo repair.

Thanks to advanced scanner technology from MicroTek, this damaged photo was restored to look like new.

Before   After

Perhaps you're not a pro with photo-editing software and can't afford the cost of restoration services. Advances in scanner technology, such as the features found in the Epson Perfection 4870 Photo scanner or the HP Scanjet 4070 Photosmart scanner, make in-home photo restoration easy.

FADED PICTURES

One common problem with photos is that images seem to fade over time. You can enhance the picture at home with photo-editing programs. If photo-editing software is not your strength, many scanners will allow you to scan a photo and instantly restore the color at the touch of a button.

Lighting Conditions

Besides sharp focus, the key to quality pictures is good lighting. Whether shooting indoors or out, the following tips will help you get the best results.

MORNING

In the morning, the sun is slightly lower in the sky, producing more subdued colors and long shadows. The blue morning sky will give your photographs a bluish tint and is an ideal time to photograph people.

Photos: Ken Trujillo, Memory Makers

NOON

Noonday light casts harsh shadows which are less flattering for human subjects. For best results, photograph people in open, even shade. If you can't avoid direct sunlight, use fill flash to eliminate harsh shadows on people's faces.

AFTERNOON

The afternoon sun starts to become slightly softer than the hard noon sun. Light at this time makes skin tones appear warmer. As the sun shifts across the sky, avoid facing your subject directly into the sun.

EVENING

As the sun lowers in the sky, long shadows return. The red-stained sky will yield dramatic and intense photos. This time is ideal for photographing architecture, landscapes and people if you're trying to capture a golden glow.

Mastering Fill Flash

Become a master of light and shadow with the fill flash setting found on most point-and-shoot cameras. Fill flash "fills" in shadows caused by direct sunlight or illuminates subjects photographed on overcast days. To see if your camera has this feature, press the flash button a few times. It often displays a lightning bolt.

WITHOUT A FILL FLASH

Photos: Eric Wilbur, Colorado Springs, Colorado

WITH A FILL FLASH

Use this feature when the sun is casting strong shadows, when the light source is behind the subject and on gray, overcast days with dull light that causes the subject to blend into the background.

On the photo above, harsh shadows darken the boy's face, hiding his expression. This is caused by the sun, the light source, as it is behind the boy. When the photo is taken using fill flash on the photo to the left, the boy's face is brightened, his eyes are visible and his skin tone is evened.

Point of View

After lighting, the point of view or angle from which you shoot your photographs can greatly enhance your images. Point of view is simply the camera's position relative to the subject. Most photos are taken at eye level with the subject in front of the camera. However, by simply changing the point of view so you are looking up or down on the subject, you instantly add interest and character to your photographs.

EYE LEVEL

WORM'S-EYE VIEW

BIRD'S-EYE VIEW

Photos: Ken Trujillo, Memory Makers

Bird's-Eye View

Stand on a chair, walk up stairs or climb a tree or ladder to experiment with a bird's-eye view. A high viewpoint can help you isolate your subject from a distracting background. Things appear smaller, and familiar things suddenly become more interesting.

Sun Day

PHOTOGRAPH SUBJECTS FROM ABOVE

Laura developed a strong tie between her photo and the page design by adding a handcut sun above her subjects, making it look as though they are sunbathing in the design. The bird's-eye viewpoint adds to the playful feel of children on a summer day.

Laura Quartuccio, Santee, California

Supplies: *Patterned paper, decorative scissors (Provo Craft); letter template (source unknown); cardstock; vellum; brads; chalk*

Worm's-Eye View

Try a worm's-eye view by taking pictures from below your subject. This viewpoint enhances the size of your subject and conveys a sense of dignity, strength or importance. Photographing upward from a low viewpoint also helps you introduce foreground elements that appear larger than life. When shooting up at buildings or trees, you'll notice that vertical lines appear to converge toward the top of the photo.

Making Tracks
PHOTOGRAPH SUBJECTS FROM BELOW

Kelli used wavy corrugated cardstock and black stamping ink to simulate tire tracks, drawing attention to the single photo. The upward angle of the photo frames the subjects with the blue sky and makes them appear larger and stronger.

Kelli Noto, Centennial, Colorado
Photo: Eric Wilbur, Colorado Springs, Colorado

Supplies: *Corrugated cardstock (DMD); letter stamps (Wordsworth); large eyelet (Creative Imaginations); stamping ink; embossing powder; cardstock*

View From Behind

Catch an unexpected expression or capture the scenery that is holding your subject's attention by shooting from behind or over the shoulder. This point of view often evokes a reflective, quiet feeling.

PHOTOGRAPHY

For This I Am Thankful

TAKE A PHOTO FROM BEHIND A SUBJECT

Sarah wanted a special page to highlight this photo of her father and 8-month-old son. The angle she chose for the photo captures a tender moment that a posed shot would not reveal.

Sarah Larson, Telford, Pennsylvania

Supplies: *Letter stamps (PSX Design); fibers (Bernat); cardstock; vellum; stamping ink; embroidery floss; eyelets; handmade paper*

Getting Creative

Grab your camera and your favorite subject and play with point of view. Don't limit yourself to bird's-eye view, worm's-eye view or views from behind. Experiment with some of the viewpoints shown here or create your own.

KNEEL DOWN

Angling the camera to the side and just slightly below her subject, the photographer was able to evoke a quiet strength in this picture of her son.

Photo: Kelli Noto, Centennial, Colorado

GET LOW

Take your camera down to the level of your pet and explore a view of the world at his or her level.

Photo: Ron Nichols, Albany, Oregon

LOOK UP

Remember laying flat in the grass and watching the clouds? Try this with a camera in hand. Get into the soccer team huddle or prepare to be snowballed.

Photo: Kelli Noto, Centennial, Colorado

CATCH A REFLECTION

If the subject gazes into a reflective item, shoot the reflection rather than the subject's face for an interesting perspective.

Photo: Deb Clover, St. Michael, Minnesota

OVER THE SHOULDER

This viewpoint created focus on the two boys' faces. From this location, the photographer was also able to back his subjects with the playing field, rather than a nondescript background.

Photo: Eric Wilbur, Colorado Springs, Colorado

ADD AN ANGLE

A diagonal tilt will convey a sense of speed, movement or action.

Photo: Ken Trujillo, Memory Makers

GET CLOSE

If a single flower is the main subject, get close with a macro setting or lens to capture the detail.

Photo: Jacque La Cour, Lochbuie, Colorado

Taking Close-Ups

Of course you remember Grandma's house, but you especially remember the porcelain candy dish full of goodies on her 1930s Art Deco coffee table. Detail shots capture the minutiae that can get overlooked in the big picture. Add historical value and develop memories with more personality and intimate perspective by taking close-up shots.

Photos: Kelli Noto, Centennial, Colorado

This Day at the Beach
ADD BEACH CLOSE-UPS

Close-up shots of all things encountered by beachcombers instill detailed memories of playtime and special relationships.

Tammy Whiting,
Colorado Springs, Colorado

Supplies: *Cardstock*

The Elements of Chloe
FOCUS ON DETAILS OF A CHILD

Close-up shots of a child's features and favorite shoes are perfect for a "pieces of you" page.

Annie Wheatcraft, Frankfort, Kentucky

Supplies: *Letter stickers (Creative Imaginations); cardstock*

Grandpa Samrah's
INCLUDE DETAILS OF A LOCATION

Each detail photo on this page flips up to reveal the stories behind the images.

Natalie Abbott, Lakewood, Colorado

Supplies: *Cardstock; vellum; eyelets; twine*

Taking Portraits

A portrait is a great way to capture one's personality and character. It can be communicated through a close-up of the face or expressed through body language in a full-figure shot, as shown here. The background can be pertinent to telling a story, but it should never compete with the person; it should be simple and visually appealing. If the background is a bit busy, you can de-emphasize it by shooting with a shallow depth of field, which will make it look out of focus. Keep the following tips in mind for taking great portraits.

Photo: Ken Trujillo, Memory Makers

3/4 FIGURE SHOT

To include the subject's background while minimizing it, try a ¾-figure shot. This type of portrait emphasizes the subject by showing most of the body and still a fair amount of the background.

Photos: Ken Trujillo, Memory Makers

HEAD SHOT

To show personality through your subject's face, shoot a head shot. A head shot is a close-up that completely fills the frame, revealing only a hint of the background.

HEAD TILTS

A tilt of the head and shoulders, forming an "s" is a feminine pose. A "c"-shaped curve of the body is a pose that works well for both men and women.

Taking Self-Portraits

There are many different ways to put yourself in the picture. Some require special equipment such as a self-timer or cable release, while others need the help of a willing friend or even a child. Regardless of the camera you own, you can and should include yourself in your photographs and your scrapbooks.

Photos: Kelli Noto, Centennial, Colorado

PHOTOS IN THE MIRROR

Use a household mirror to take a picture of yourself. It is best to disable the camera's flash so that it doesn't show in the reflective surface. You'll need a bright room and faster film (ISO 400 or higher). Or, take a mirror outdoors for your self-portrait.

When outside, stay in the shade or take the photographs later in the day when the sun is low and the shadows on your face will be soft. Look at your image in the mirror through the camera's lens and compose and focus accordingly. Move the camera away from your face, point it toward your reflection in the mirror, hold the camera as steady as possible and take the picture. The camera will be in the photo, but the photo can easily be cropped so that only your face is showing.

Self-Portrait Alternative

Use these tips to help capture your photo.

GIVE A QUICK LESSON

Even a young child is capable of handling a camera. When a child takes a picture of an adult from the child's eye level, unflattering distortion can occur. Have the child stand on a chair or even a table to gain a more flattering vantage point. As an alternative, sit on the ground to put yourself level with a camera in the hands of a child.

USE A DIGITAL CAMERA

Have your photo taken with a digital camera so you can immediately see the results.

The first couple of shots showed more of the lawn than the subject, but after a quick lesson and a little practice with the subject's 5-year-old friend, a great photo was captured.

SELF-TIMERS AND REMOTES

Many cameras have timers or remote-control devices that help with self-portraits. Steady the camera with a tripod or even a stack of books. Look through the lens to where you will be and frame the picture. Most cameras have an auto-focus feature that focuses on the object in the center of the frame where you'll be standing. Carefully set the timer without moving the camera and get into place. You could also use a remote control device, which allows you to snap the picture when you feel ready. If you feel awkward in front of the camera, try engaging in an activity as shown at right. This offers a distraction from the camera, and allows you to capture yourself doing something you enjoy.

Photos: Kelli Noto, Centennial, Colorado

Taking Group Portraits

Group photographs can be difficult. The arrangement sometimes looks cluttered as everyone squashes together to fit into the photo, and taller people can block the shorter ones. Resist the temptation to line everyone up. Try the basic triangle composition method and relationship rule as in the photos below. Organizing people in clusters by relationship adds warmth to a photo. Traditional or inverted triangle shapes formed by people of varying heights will add visual interest and ensure no one is obstructed.

Photos: Ken Trujillo, Memory Makers

TRIANGLE CLUSTERS

Triangle clusters create closeness, and the shot can be cropped either vertically or horizontally.

USING A BENCH

This group shot utilizes a bench as a tool to vary heights. You could easily add two more people by having them kneel in front of the bench.

STAGGERING

Heights were staggered for this arrangement, employing the triangle composition method.

STAGGERED LINE

This casual, staggered line of three makes for a spontaneous photo with everyone in close proximity. This shot can be cropped vertically.

TRIANGLE

A triangle is easily formed with a group of three and can be cropped universally. This succeeds as everyone's face is seen, the frame is filled and the focus is on the people.

SIDEWAYS LINE

A line-up sideways and shot on an angle is visually appealing and can be cropped horizontally. It is good to use a prop, such as a railing.

Creating a Home Studio

As scrapbookers become more experienced and invest in better equipment, many are interested in setting up home studios for more professional-looking shots. Creating a home photo studio requires only a few simple adjustments and a cleared corner of your home that benefits from natural light. Costs for setting up the studio are low, and the more comfortable the photo subject is, the better chance of capturing candid, spontaneous moments.

HOME STUDIO SETUP

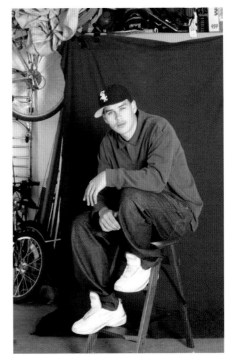

1 Find a space with good natural light (but not direct sunlight), such as the garage, and clear it out.

2 Purchase fabric to use as a backdrop and secure it behind your cleared area. Pose your subject approximately three feet from the backdrop.

3 Position yourself a few feet from the subject and begin snapping. If necessary, use a piece of white foam core, a full-length mirror or a sheet as a reflector.

4 Get the film developed and enjoy your professional-quality photos.

Photos: Kelli Noto, Centennial, Colorado

Tips For Taking Great Photos

Sensational photos are the hallmark of every scrapbook page. Whether the images are of people, places or things, good photographs are the result of careful composition, attention to lighting and tenacity. Try these tips for spicing up the visual interest in your images.

Birthday Parties

BLOWING OUT THE CANDLES

Use the flash for this action shot. The camera's shutter slows without the flash, which results in blurry action shots.

Photos: Kelli Noto, Centennial, Colorado

PERSON WITH CAKE

To use the candles' glow as light, turn off the flash (and make sure the cake is a safe distance from the subject's face). The balloons add to the visual context of this photo.

PARTY ACTIVITIES

Use fast film (400 speed) to photograph moving bodies. Frame both the person and the elements of the activity (boy and piñata) in the viewfinder to help tell the full story for candid activity shots.

4th of July

CANDID MOMENTS

To capture the feel of the Fourth, shoot candid moments typical of family celebrations. Kids and sparklers are best photographed at dusk when there is still enough light to see excited faces clearly. Experiment with shutter speeds to catch the color and shine of the main event—the fireworks show.

Photos: Kelli Noto, Centennial, Colorado

PATRIOTIC PORTRAIT

Make time to take a few posed shots during the Fourth of July festivities. To avoid squinty or shadowy eyes that are often a result of bright sun, position your subject fully in even shade.

Halloween

GREAT PUMPKINS

While photographing the pumpkin carving is pretty straightforward, it can be difficult to capture the glowing effect of a jack-o'-lantern. Try diffusing the camera's flash and placing an extra candle or two inside the jack-o'-lantern for added illumination.

SHOOTING THE LOOT

While you are capturing the many events of Halloween night, don't forget to photograph the candy and trinkets collected during trick-or-treating.

Photos: Kelli Noto, Centennial, Colorado

Photo: Jacque La Cour, Lochbuie, Colorado

Christmas

PERSON IN FRONT OF THE TREE

Lighting is important when taking a photo of a person in front of a Christmas tree. If you want the person to appear in silhouette, turn off the flash. Use the camera's strobe to make the person's face visible. To show the glow of the lights, try to balance the light in the room with that of the tree.

Photos: Kelli Noto, Centennial, Colorado

HOLIDAY LIGHTS

The best time to take photos of outside lights is just as it starts to get dark and before the sky goes black. But if you have a house that is covered with lights or a public display that is quite bright, the lights will provide enough detail that the time of night becomes less important. Turn off the flash and keep the camera as steady as possible.

Photographing the Tree

NO LIGHTS AND NO FLASH

Taken at night with no flash and only the tree lights on, the darkness masks the twinkle lights, ornaments and definition of the tree.

ROOM LIGHTS AND FLASH

With flash and the room lights on, this photo shows the tree in detail, but the brightness washes out the glow of the twinkle lights.

NO LIGHTS AND FLASH

The soft effect of this photo was achieved by bouncing the camera's flash off of the ceiling, providing subtle light and a little more glow. A layer of tissues over the camera's flash will have the same effect.

ROOM LIGHTS AND NO FLASH

The room lights were left on and no flash was used for this photo that shows detail of the tree, twinkle lights and ornaments in a soft orange glow.

Photos: Kelli Noto, Centennial, Colorado

Chapter

Page Design and Layout

In the world of graphic arts, good design communicates a message in an attractive, impactful way. When you design scrapbook pages, the goal is the same. The choices you make when arranging photos, choosing embellishments and including text should convey the true spirit of a certain moment in time, whether it is the birth of a child or a day at an amusement park. When you employ the design concepts discussed in this chapter, you will start thinking like a graphic designer, and the artful results will translate to your scrapbook layouts.

Discover Photo Inspiration

Let your photographs serve as the basis for page design inspiration.

Every great layout begins with the best photos. Selecting the strongest photos helps stir memories, evoke emotions or relive treasured moments. Eliminating the weaker photos helps make the design process even easier.

Start this selection process by spreading all possibilities in front of you and sorting them into two categories: good photos and not-so-good photos. What is considered a good photo? One that makes you smile or sigh or evokes a memory. A photo that is out of focus, has a subject with closed eyes or feels visually cluttered is instantly eliminated.

Next, analyze the good photos. Compare similar shots to see if one stands out above the rest. For example, the photographer of the baseball photos on page 77 had several her of son at bat. In one, he stands just waiting for the pitch. In others, he is swinging the bat, but the ball isn't visible. In another, you can tell by the location of the ball that he swung and missed. Then there is one where he is swinging as the ball approaches, capturing the action of the sport and the determination on the boy's face at the same time. This photo was chosen as the focal point of the spread.

Do the same analysis to choose the page's secondary photos. Of all the photos of her son wearing his catcher's mask, the photographer chose one in which his eyes are visible and his tongue is out in concentration. Continue this process of elimination to choose other photos for the page at different angles and distances.

When Kevin was six, he played coach-pitch baseball. He liked batting the most, but despised playing catcher. When he was catching, he squatted behind the plate as the ball pummeled him time after time. "They should call it backstop instead of catcher," Kevin said. Kevin also spent a lot of time in the outfield and would daydream or pick at the grass knowing that the ball had very little chance of ever making it out that far. Kevin liked that his t-shirt was purple because it was the same color as the Colorado Rockies.

Play Ball!

Kevin

Play Ball
USE A SYSTEM TO CHOOSE THE BEST PHOTOS

Kelli turned the large pile of photos she had into a home-run layout by using a system to narrow down photos. Her ultimate favorite became the inspiration for her design as well as the focal point of the spread.

Kelli Noto, Centennial, Colorado

Supplies: *Patterned paper (Colorbök); die-cut letters(QuicKutz); circle cutter (Creative Memories); cardstock; transparency*

Clarify the Message

Once you've chosen the right photos for your page, it's time to find your journaling angle.

PAGE DESIGN

Concentrating on journaling early in the design process means you're focusing on your scrapbook page as a complete package. The angle you decide to take with your writing and the words you choose truly impact the rest of the page. If the tone of the journaling is fun, you can go with a playful design and bright colors. But if the journaling is more serious, you may want to opt for muted tones or more open space.

Thinking about your journaling before putting your page together remedies the problems of running out of space or missing an opportunity to include all of the details. It also means that each part of your page will work with and support the other parts, and you'll end up with pages that tell the whole story in a clever and creative way.

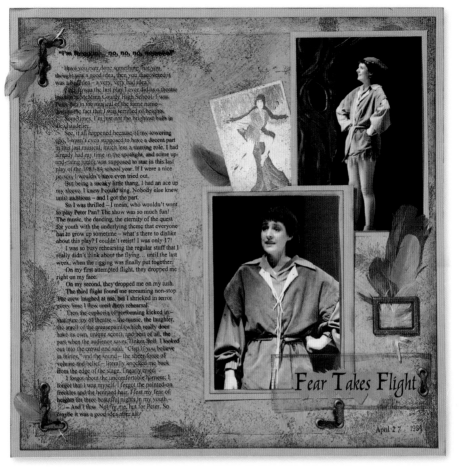

Fear Takes Flight
PLAN SPACE FOR AN INTERESTING STORY

Without the journaling, viewers of this page would have no idea that Bay shrieked during all of the flying scenes in her high school production of "Peter Pan." Bay planned the journaling for this page in advance so she could allow enough room to tell the story, which she writes using her own voice and plenty of vivid descriptions.

Bay Loftis, Philadelphia, Tennessee

Supplies: *Textured stamp (Club Scrap); date stamp (Making Memories); cardstock; transparency; stamping inks; embossing powder; eyelets; concho; acrylic paint; feathers; chalk; fibers; frame*

Create a Color Concept

Use the inspiration of your photos and the message of your journaling to help select the right color scheme.

The color wheel is a guide to color selection. It is divided into sections of primary colors (yellow, blue and red), secondary colors (found in between the primaries: green, violet and orange), and tertiary colors (mixtures of primary and secondary colors: yellow-green, blue-green, blue-violet, red-violet, red-orange and yellow-orange). The wheel can show you which colors make great combinations based on their placement. For example, three colors spaced equidistant from one another on the wheel—like red, yellow and blue—form a triadic color scheme as shown on the following page. An analogous color scheme can be formed by choosing colors that are right next to each other on the wheel. Hold this handy tool up to your photos to determine the color scheme that will best suit your page and theme. The choices are endless, and it will help you create no-fail color combinations every time.

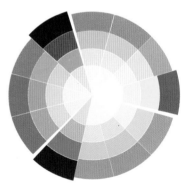

PAGE DESIGN

Enjoy Life
USE A TRIADIC COLOR SCHEME

Jennifer selected a triadic color scheme of red, blue and yellow for this page based on the red that is present in her subject's clothing and soda bottle. She chose less intense shades to keep the photo at center stage and create the rustic feeling of a young boy at the beach. Bottle-cap accents coordinate with the color scheme as well as the photo's content.

Jennifer Bourgeault, Macomb Township, Michigan

Supplies: *Patterned paper (Daisy D's); dimensional adhesive (JudiKins); bottle caps (Li'l Davis Designs); letter stickers (EK Success, Me & My Big Ideas); poemstones stickers (Creative Imaginations); stamping ink; cardstock*

Assemble the Layout

Once you have all the elements—photos, words, colors and materials—it's time to design your layout.

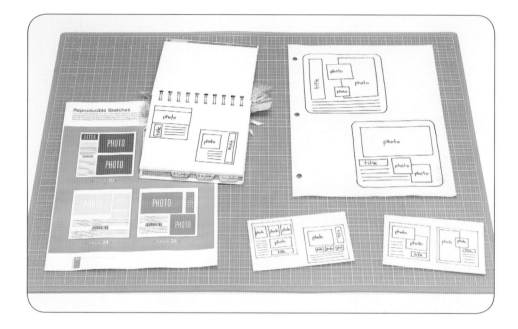

Finding the right arrangement for your page elements is the final step in the design process, but often this is the most challenging part. It can help to sketch sample layouts on paper first or turn to scrapbook publications that include ready-made sketch ideas. This will give you a realistic idea of the exact amount of space you have for photos, journaling and other accents and help you to arrange those pieces accordingly. For example, maybe you've selected silk flowers and fern punches as page accents, but the sketch you want to use allows one block for embellishment. To better suit the space, add the items to a decorated tag, as shown left.

Trudy Sigurdson, Victoria, British Columbia, Canada

Supplies: *Letter stickers (source unknown); paper flowers (Making Memories); fern punch (Punch Bunch); metal accents (source unknown); patterned fabric; lace trim; cardstock; vellum; stamping ink; thread; tag; fiber*

Elements of Design

Consider the five basic components of line, color, space, texture and shape to design visually appealing layouts.

Line

Lines create shape and form. Their edges, whether straight, crooked, clean or fuzzy, contribute to the overall feel of a page. They work solo or in conjunction with other lines or shapes to organize, create movement or textures, and guide the eye throughout the design.

soft

curvilinear

geometric

straight & clean

PAGE DESIGN

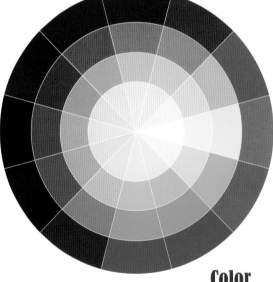

Color

Color immediately draws the eye, eliciting an emotional response. Because of this power, color is an important design element that can establish a mood and greatly add to a composition.

Space

Space is the area in which a design is created and interacts. In scrapbooking, your page background has its own space and each component of the design—photos, journaling blocks, embellishments etc.—has its own positive space that stands alone. Those elements interact to form other spaces, both positive and negative. Positive space, first catching the eye, is in the forefront, and negative space is in the background.

Texture

Texture is the surface quality of an element that can be either tactile or visual. It adds depth, dimension and visual interest to a page. Texture can set a mood such as rugged with corrugated cardboard or romantic with luxurious velvet. A matte surface can offer conservative and understated tones whereas a metallic surface can mean glitzy and bold. The whisper of sparkle on an iridescent surface can lend itself to fancy or feminine.

Shape

Shapes can be organic as found in nature, geometric and hard-edged or anywhere in between. Their purpose is to guide the eye, set a tone and organize the information on the page.

Principles of Design

Employ basic design principles to your scrapbooking to dramatically improve your pages.

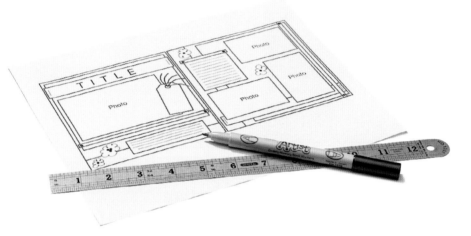

Faced with a pile of photos, paper and embellishments, even experienced scrapbookers approach page design using diverse methods. Some are "pushers" who move photos around on a page or computer screen until they are happy with the design. Some are "sketchers" who draw their layouts with pencil and paper before even one photo is cropped. Others are "dreamers" who create mental layouts all the time—whether at home, on the go or even while snapping photographs. But great pages don't depend on adopting a particular method, they rely upon principles of design. With certain design principles at work, pushers, sketchers and dreamers alike can create great pages regardless of their methods.

It only takes a few minutes to learn the basic principles of design. And it only takes the next cropping session to begin to use them more deliberately in your layouts. These principles—emphasis, rhythm, balance and unity—are the four "secrets" for great design.

Like stacks of children's blocks, your scrapbook layouts will fall flat if not properly balanced—with design principles, that is. Developing a conscious understanding of certain design principles and using them on your layouts will keep this from happening. The principles of emphasis, rhythm, balance and unity are discussed on the next few pages. Understanding them will give you confidence in the design choices you make and allow you to produce stunning layouts that preserve your cherished memories.

Create Emphasis

To create emphasis, you must first define the purpose and message of your layout. What do you want to communicate? How do you want the page to feel? The answers to these questions determine the focal point. Usually it is the best or most important photo, but it might be another element such as a piece of memorabilia or a written story. Once you've selected a focal point, determine how you will emphasize it. Emphasis is often created through size, with larger items becoming more important than smaller ones. But you can also emphasize with color, repetition, line, shape, texture, contrast or other details. For example, bright colors tend to dominate more subdued tones. A photo cropped into an interesting shape will draw attention as well.

...Dat Moon

Dana emphasized her photo by cropping with strong angles and layering a light-colored photo mat over two darker mats, thereby drawing attention with contrast. She also placed the photo in the layout's "sweet spot," or slightly away from the center.

Dana Swords, Doswell, Virginia

Supplies: *Patterned paper (K & Company); metallic paper (DMD); star stickers (EK Success); metallic thread (DMC); cardstock*

Think Pink
USE SHAPE TO CREATE EMPHASIS

Kari created a focal point by cropping her best flamingo photo into a circle. As the only large round element on the page, it draws the viewer's attention first and contrasts with the rectangles elsewhere in the design. The central flamingo photo is further emphasized with a white mat and by overlapping it with part of the title.

Kari Hansen, Memory Makers magazine

Supplies: Patterned papers (EK Success, Paper Company); transparency (Grafix); flamingo stamp (Inkadinkado); flower stamps (Stamps by Judith); postmark stamp cube (Stampington & Co.); watercolor paints (Canson); faux postage stamps (Provo Craft); photo corners (Kolo); cardstock; tags; buttons; ribbons; trim; sandpaper; stamping ink; thread; foam tape

Foolproof Focal Points

Using your favorite photo as the focus of your layout is easy when you use one of these tips or techniques to create a strong focal point.

PAGE DESIGN

- Enlarge the main photo for maximum visual effect. Try a 5 x 7" or 6 x 9" photo, or be dramatic and use a full-page panoramic.

- Mat the photo with a color that is in high contrast to the page background color scheme.

- Orient the focal photo differently than the supporting photos. Tilt it if all the rest are straight, make it horizontal among predominant verticals, etc.

- Crop the main photo into a contrasting shape, such as an oval or circle, to play against the rectangular shapes of the other photos.

- Decorate the focal photo in a distinct manner. Add multilayered mats, textured papers, special photo corners, ribbons or shiny accents to draw attention to it.

- Use a close-up shot as the focal point. It will have more impact than photos with distant subjects.

Your Left Foot
CREATE FOCAL POINT WITH A PHOTO ENLARGEMENT

The dominant and subordinate elements in this layout allow the reader's eye to move smoothly from the super-sized photo to the tag title and then to the story. In addition, the unusual subject matter of the photo draws viewers in and makes them want to know more.

Susan Cyrus, Broken Arrow, Oklahoma

Supplies: *Patterned papers (Creative Imaginations, Karen Foster Design, Wordsworth); tag (Designer's Library); phrase sticker (Me & My Big Ideas); footprint stickers (EK Success); quote sticker (Memories Complete); letter stamps (All Night Media); footprint stamp (Stamp Craft); stamping ink; chalk; pen; staple; denim; shoelace*

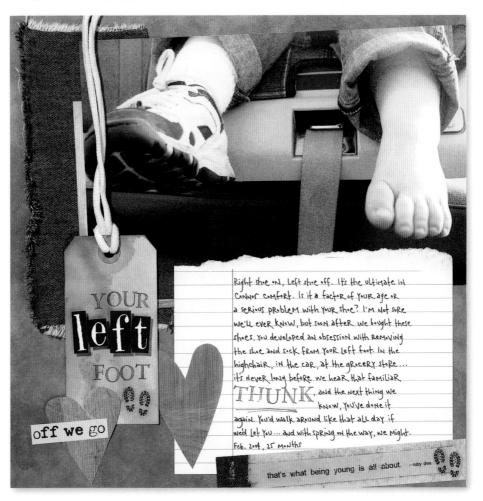

Right shoe on, Left shoe off. It's the ultimate in Connor comfort. Is it a factor of your age or a serious problem with your shoe? I'm not sure we'll ever know, but soon after we bought these shoes, you developed an obsession with removing the shoe and sock from your Left foot. In the highchair, in the car, at the grocery store... it's never long before we hear that familiar THUNK, and the next thing we know, you've done it again. You'd walk around like that all day if we'd let you... and with spring on the way, we might. Feb. 2004, 25 months

that's what being young is all about. — ruby dee

Produce Rhythm

While rhythm is a term most commonly associated with music, there is a specific formula for creating visual rhythm within design. Rhythm results from a pattern with both repetition and variation of shape, size, color, line, texture or other details. It creates the illusion of movement or motion, which in turn adds energy and excitement to your scrapbook pages. There are many ways to produce rhythm on your layouts. You can use multiple shades of one color, repeat the same photo in different sizes, include a series of similar shapes along a straight line or create a pattern with lines of different weights spaced irregularly. You'll note that in all these examples, something is repeated, yet within the repetition, there is something different about each element. This is the key concept to remember when creating rhythm yourself.

Z Is for Zoe

Melanie's page shows a good use of rhythm by highlighting Zoe's red hat throughout the design. The red patterned paper mirrors the hat tassel while circle alphabet stamps repeated throughout the journaling text echo the circular shape. Nubby fibers mirror the knitted texture of the hat. The page is unified and the eye travels smoothly over the page.

Melanie Bauer, Columbia, Missouri

Supplies: Patterned papers (Chatterbox, Li'l Davis Designs); textured paper (Bazzill); letter stamps (PSX Design); metal frame (Making Memories); woven label (Me & My Big Ideas); stamping ink; fiber; pen

David has always wanted to try woodworking. His senior year of college, he finally got the chance. All semester, I knew he was working on something special. He wouldn't tell me what it was, but I got updates on how it was going. He'd tell me he got the best pieces of wood and what type of tools he was learning to use. I could tell he loved working with his hands. He told me that he was making my Christmas present. I was so interested to know what it was. He's so good at keeping a secret, that I was shocked when he spilled the beans on his last day of class. He was bragging and said, "I got a perfect score on my clock." I pretended that I missed it, but I was secretly rejoicing. I love clocks. But what I wasn't prepared for was what a truly beautiful job he'd done. When I opened it on Christmas day I could hardly contain the emotion. From the broken swan-neck pediment down to the hand-carved shell motif at the bottom, and the two toned wood, his clock was a work of art. The wood was a beautiful walnut, stained and crafted to perfection. No one would ever guess that this beautiful clock, my beautiful clock, is the first thing he ever built. I will cherish it always, and I know it will be one of the most sought after heirlooms we leave. Every time I look at it, I'm reminded of how much my husband loves me.

My Beautiful Clock
CREATE RHYTHM WITH SHAPES AND COLOR

Many examples of rhythm exist on this page. Kara started by using three different shades of brown. For the title, she repeated an angled block shape along a straight line. She added black brads to the background diamond pattern and different-sized photos with even spaces in between each.

Kara Henry, Orem, Utah

Supplies: *Patterned papers (Provo Craft, SEI); stamping ink; cardstock; brads*

Foolproof Rhythm

If you use an element once, repeat it in the layout. For example, if you use gingham ribbon at the top of a tag, include it in the title or along the corners of your photos as well. The eye will automatically connect related objects that create a pattern.

It is especially effective to use recurring elements in ways that create a visual shape, such as a triangle or quadrangle. The eye will travel the implied path of these shapes, establishing movement throughout the design.

friends

PAULA, ABBIE

happy

friends

...and in the sweetness of friendship, let there be laughter and sharing of pleasures. ~ Kahil Gibran
I hope throughout your life you continue to find good friends to share good times with. ~ mom

fun

summer·03

Thetis Lake Victoria
ACHIEVE MOVEMENT WITH CIRCLES AND RECTANGLES

The pattern of wide rectangles across this spread creates rhythm while emphasizing the ex-
pansiveness of the lake. Repeated colored circles interspersed with bright daisies intensifies
the feeling of movement.

Sharon Whitehead, Vernon, British Columbia, Canada

Supplies: *Metal words (Making Memories); circle cut-outs (Scrapworks); letter stickers (Chatterbox); flower accents (Paper House Productions); foam tape; cardstock*

Achieve Balance

To apply the concept of balance in scrapbooking, imagine a vertical line running down the center of your page. Assess the page elements placed on the left and right sides of this line. Does one side have significantly more elements than the other, causing one side to feel too heavy or too light? Do the same with a horizontal line. Does the page feel top-heavy? Once you've put your page to this test, you may need to rearrange some elements in order to balance the page. Thus, it's a good idea to perform this test before the adhering everything to the background. The more you are aware of proper balance, the easier arranging page elements will become.

Some Thoughts From Your Mother

Joy achieves symmetrical balance with a reversed mirror-image design. The photo on the top and the text on the bottom of one page is reversed on the other, and therefore balance each other.

Joy Bohon, Bedford, Indiana

Supplies: *Textured papers (Bazzill); letter stickers, molding plaque (Chatterbox); brads*

The Mickey Pool

BALANCE THE PLACEMENT OF DESIGN ELEMENTS

Large black circles placed in opposite corners of Jennifer's layout help to balance her page. The circles are balanced even though they are different sizes because one is filled with the weighty detail of a photograph while the other is filled with light color and small type. The title is large yet airy, which balances the solid rectangular photo of the boy.

Jennifer Bourgeault, Macomb Township, Michigan

Supplies: *Letter stickers (Sticker Studio); epoxy letter accents (Creative Imaginations); circle cutter (Provo Craft); patterned vellum (American Crafts); tag (Making Memories); Mickey stamp (source unknown); cardstock; brads*

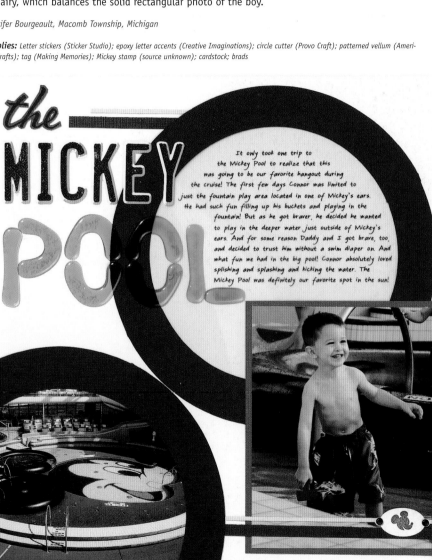

It only took one trip to the Mickey Pool to realize that this was going to be our favorite hangout during the cruise! The first few days Connor was limited to just the fountain play area located in one of Mickey's ears. He had such fun filling up his buckets and playing in the fountain! But as he got braver, he decided he wanted to play in the deeper water just outside of Mickey's ears. And for some reason Daddy and I got brave, too, and decided to trust him without a swim diaper on. And what fun we had in the big pool! Connor absolutely loved splashing and splashing and kicking the water. The Mickey Pool was definitely our favorite spot in the sun!

Methods of Balance

There are several different types of balance and ways it can be achieved. Symmetrical balance, often considered more orderly or formal, occurs when like shapes are repeated in the exact same positions on either side of a center axis. For asymmetrical balance, the more casual or playful method, dissimilar objects are arranged in different ways on either side of a center point. Yet another type is radial balance, where design elements spiral outward from a common center point. The method of balance you use on scrapbook layouts will depend on the number and type of page accents you have and the mood you wish to achieve. Study these examples to help select the best fit for your design.

PAGE DESIGN

SYMMETRICAL/BILATERAL

If folded down the center, each side is a mirror image of the other.

ASYMMETRICAL BY TEXTURE

The tactile nature of the fabric and button adds detail to the center, making it equally weighty as the images above and below.

ASYMMETRICAL BY COLOR

Light-colored paper strips and buttons contrast nicely with the dark-colored outlines around the bottom images.

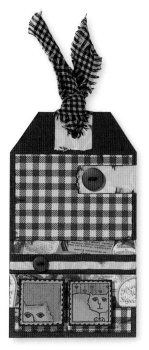

ASYMMETRICAL BY SHAPE

A smaller shape balances the weight of a larger one due to its playful form and dark outline.

RADIAL

All lines and buttons originate from the accent in the center.

ASYMMETRICAL BY POSITION

A button on bright paper was placed off-center to balance the visual weight of stamped images on the bottom.

All tags by Kari Hansen,
Memory Makers magazine

Attain Unity

Unity has been acheived when all elements of a page look like they belong together. Unified elements will help your page look complete. Many elements including shape, size, color, texture, line and pattern can contribute to unity, and there are many ways to create it. You could choose a color scheme and stick to it. Select only one or two lettering styles for all the text on a page. Use a border or other linear design around a two-page spread. Crop all your photos to the same size. Repeat a shape, color or texture across a page (see p. 101). It's really a concept you practice every day as you get dressed. You might select slacks to match one of the colors in a patterned shirt, then add coordinating earrings, a necklace or shoes. Keep the same mind-set as you create pages for cohesive results every time.

Reflections

Jennifer accomplishes unity in her layout by grouping and repeating block shapes. The layered shapes help move the reader's eye around the page. The placement of her photos with the subject looking down or toward the center keeps the eye from running off the page.

Jennifer Lamb, Rolesville, North Carolina

Supplies: Textured papers (Bazzill); botanical stickers (source unknown); faux wax seal (Creative Imaginations); vellum

One beautiful sunny day.
One big purple dinosaur.
One sweet, delicious cake.
One yard full of family and friends.
All for...
One adorable baby on the day she turned ONE.

Kristen
June 1999

One
UNIFY A PAGE WITH SHAPE AND COLOR

Lisa Dixon repeated a candle shape across the bottom of her page to give it a complete, unified look. In addition, she stuck to only two main colors—yellow and blue—and included those colors in various ways all across her page. The repeated number 1 clustered around the title also creates unity while accentuating the birthday theme.

Lisa Dixon, East Brunswick, New Jersey

Supplies: *Patterned paper (PrintWorks); textured cardstocks (Bazzill); die-cut letters and candle (Sizzix); date stamp (Making Memories); vellum; chalk; paint chips*

Unity Made Easy

There are lots of different ways you can unify pages. For a single page, unify by repeating a certain embellishment or color in different areas. For a spread, let your title or a shape cross the gutter between the two pages. For a theme album, use the same or a very similar layout for each page. Then, create a title and ending page that look similar as well.

Summer 2003

USE LINES AND SQUARES TO UNIFY A SPREAD

On this spread, a strong horizontal line of patterned paper running through the center unifies both pages. Groupings of brightly colored squares placed in different areas also pulls the design together nicely, while adding a playful touch.

Angie Head, Friendswood, Texas

Supplies: *Patterned paper (Sandylion); phrase stickers, letter stamps (Wordsworth); epoxy stickers (EK Success); cardstock; stamping ink*

Elements of Success

Chances are you have some layouts that you like better than others in your albums. Similarly, when you read scrapbook magazines or look through your friends' albums, there's no doubt that certain pages stand out as especially well-done. While personal taste plays a part in what draws you to certain pages, there are several basic components that can make any layout eye-catching. A successful layout is definitely a package deal. On the next few pages, you can evaluate the elements. You'll see how the presence, or sometimes the absence, of certain design elements separates a so-so layout from a great one.

PAGE DESIGN

Self-Evaluation Guide

ASK YOURSELF THESE 11 QUESTIONS TO DETERMINE THE SUCCESS OF YOUR LAYOUT:

1. *Does my title lure the viewer and elicit interest?*

2. *Is my journaling legible, tidy, and does it express my theme?*

3. *Are there stray pencil marks, crooked elements, visible adhesive or other craftsmanship issues?*

4. *Are my photos aesthetically sound, relevant to my story and of good quality?*

5. *Do the colors complement the photos and fit with the tone of the layout?*

6. *Do my embellishments add to the theme of the page or detract from it?*

7. *Do the embellishments emphasize my photos or overwhelm them?*

8. *Are there any floating elements?*

9. *Does the eye move through the design or is the layout static or confusing?*

10. *Do all the parts of the layout flow together as a cohesive whole?*

11. *Does the layout tell the story I want to convey?*

No journaling, weak title

Unbalanced composition with no focal point

Patterns distract from photos rather than complement

No contrast in color values

Design confuses the eye; floating elements

UNSUCCESSFUL LAYOUT

While the individual pieces on this layout are attractive and trendy, when combined, they conflict. The lack of balance and contrast causes the photos to be buried in a chaotic design. The absence of journaling and a strong title results in a layout that lacks meaning.

Supplies: *Patterned paper (Hot Off The Press); pumpkin eyelets (source unknown); beaded pumpkin stickers (Colorbök); typewriter stickers (EK Success); rickrack; cardstock*

Title is stronger but lacks interest

No clear focal point

Patterns all similar scale, makes page feel busy

Impersonal journaling has little impact

Color choices are better, but predictable; still lack spark

AVERAGE LAYOUT

On this layout, the combination of colors and embellishments has improved, however, they are still not totally pleasing. While the layout design is balanced and has some interesting elements, it still lacks a dynamic composition and fresh approach.

Supplies: *Patterned papers (Bo-Bunny Press, EK Success); textured paper (Bazzill); border stickers (Pebbles); leaf tags (EK Success); letter template (C-Thru Ruler); button (Making Memories); foam tape; cardstock*

Colors complement
photos and carry
out theme

Playful,
personal,
accessible
journaling

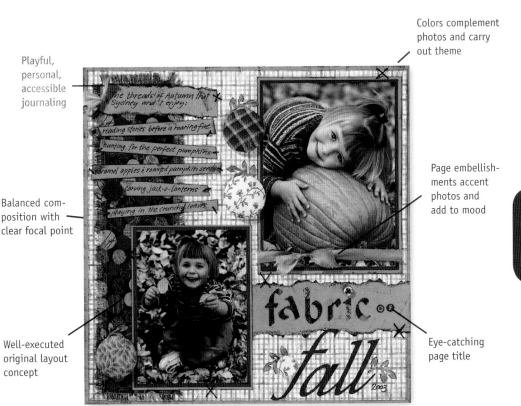

Page embellish-
ments accent
photos and
add to mood

Balanced com-
position with
clear focal point

PAGE DESIGN

Well-executed
original layout
concept

Eye-catching
page title

SUCCESSFUL LAYOUT

This layout succeeds due to: 1. Great photos that take center stage; 2. A
title and personal journaling that draw in the viewer and add to the story
of the page; 3. A balanced composition and clear focal point; 4. Rich colors and textures that evoke the spirit of fall; 5. Originality and neatness
in execution.

All designs by Kari Hansen, Memory Makers magazine

Supplies: *Patterned paper (Bo-Bunny Press); textured paper (Bazzill); fabrics (Jo-Ann Stores); covered
button kits (Prym-Dritz); leaf punch (EK Success); letter die cuts (QuicKutz); letter stamps (PSX Design);
fiber (Timeless Touches); ribbon (Artchix Studio); dye ink (Ranger); fabric stabilizer (Therm O Web); buttons (ScrapArts); hole punch (McGill); pen; cardstock; thread*

Chapter

Creative Techniques

It seems nearly anything goes when it comes to decorating modern scrapbook pages. There is a plethora of products out there to achieve almost any look you desire, from old-fashioned to industrial. But while buying the products is one thing, learning to use them on layouts is quite another. Using simple steps, this chapter will show you how to incorporate a variety of creative techniques to achieve a specific effect or the desired look.

Creative Photo Cropping

In the most practical sense, cropping, or simply cutting the edges of your photographs, will make more room on the page for other elements and allow you to focus on the central subject of the picture. But cropping can also provide interesting design elements when more intricate methods are used. It can be just as fun and creative as designing detailed titles or handmade embellishments. Cropping can change the entire composition of your photos, allowing you to see them in a whole new light.

Photos: Kelly Angard,
Highlands Ranch, Colorado

Valerie Barton, Flowood, Mississippi

MaryJo Regier, Memory Makers Books

we left our hearts in san francisco, summer 2002

When to Crop

A photo can tell many stories depending on how it is cropped. As you experiment with photo cropping, you will become keenly aware of what types of photo cropping techniques work best for certain types of photo compositions. Put photo cropping to use in the following situations for eye-pleasing results:

COMMAND FOCUS

Busy photos with lots of people and unnecessary background elements take attention away from the photos' main subjects. Framing, slicing and silhouetting can isolate and focus attention on your subject.

CORRECT FLAWS

Cropping allows you to remove photo blemishes, such as flare from flashes, closed eyes, strangers in your pictures, out-of-focus elements, lab printing errors and more. It even allows you to use "junk" photos from the beginning of a roll of film!

BOOST STYLE

Add style and variety to your page by cropping your photos into shapes. There are many shapes with which to experiment, and changing the shape will also alter the final effect. Give your cropped photo breathing room, however, so that the photo's content is not lost.

DESIGN NEW ART

When you don't seem to have the right page accent to complement certain photographs or would like to keep the design completely focused on the photos, turn photos into new pieces of art by cropping in unique and unusual ways.

Photo: Trudy Sigurdson, Victoria, British Columbia, Canada

What a Pussycat
SLICE PHOTOS AND REASSEMBLE

Kelly made these great photos even more interesting by adding a creative photo cropping technique. She made vertical slices with a paper trimmer through different sections of her photos, being careful to leave the lion faces intact. After slicing, she reassembled the pieces on her page with even spaces in between.

Kelly Angard, Highlands Ranch, Colorado
Photos: Jeff Neal, Huntington Beach, California

Supplies: Mesh (Magic Mesh); cardstock; pen

Shadow-Cut a Self-Framing Photo

Shadow cutting a frame is an excellent way to draw your eye right into the focus of the photo while adding some interest to the framing effect itself. Jodi used a brass "shadowing" stencil to create the butterfly pattern, and an oval graduated template to crop out the center. Follow the instructions to apply this technique to your photo.

Jodi Amidei, Memory Makers Books
Photo: Chrissie Tepe, Lancaster, California

Secure photo face up to back of brass stencil with temporary adhesive. Use a craft knife to carefully cut out stencil's pattern on photo. Set aside resulting frame. Place remaining photo center on plastic foam cutting mat and top with oval graduated template and center image. Use swivel blade knife to crop photo into an oval shape. Reassemble center in frame on cardstock.

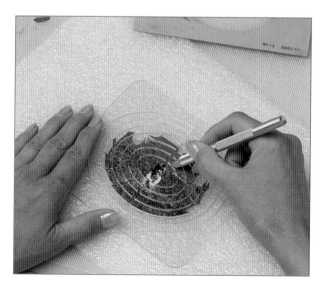

Creating Unique Backgrounds

Making page backgrounds is fun because you have more surface area to work with, resulting in many, many possibilities for background designs. You can cut or tear small pieces of paper to form a mosaic background, stamp it with letters, words or images, sand the edges, weave paper strips, thread it with ribbon and much more. Just keep in mind that color choice is important—the background should complement the colors in your photos without overpowering them.

TECHNIQUES

American Pride
CUT AND SAND SMALL SQUARES FOR A BACKGROUND

Pam punched 1½" squares from patterned paper and sanded them for a classic, time-worn, patriotic look. After the squares were finished and assembled on the background (see p. 115), Pam cut a clear-backed quote sticker to fit on squares, allowing her design to show through.

Pam Klassen, Reedley, California
Photos: Ricki Helmsing, Phoenix, Arizona and Molly Bruce, Cave Creek, Arizona

Supplies: *Patterned papers (Carolee's Creations, Chatterbox, Design Originals, Hot Off The Press, K & Company, Karen Foster Design, Magenta, Paper Patch, Papers by Catherine); letter stamps (Ma Vinci's Reliquary); dimensional paint (Delta); quote sticker (Wordsworth)*

1 Punch enough squares to cover the majority of a 12 x 12" cardstock sheet: nine from blue patterned papers and 33 from red patterned papers.

2 Rub a sanding pad around all edges of squares, creating a worn look.

3 Arrange squares on background to form a flag with all the blue squares in the top left corner. Adhere squares to page, spacing ¼" apart.

Preschool Graduate
STAMP A SCHOOL-THEMED BACKGROUND

To accompany patterned background paper on her daughter's preschool graduation page, Brandi stamped letters of the alphabet across white cardstock (see p. 117). She chose chalk ink colors that were similar to several of her paper colors.

Brandi Ginn, Longmont, Colorado

Supplies: *Patterned paper, premade tag, nails (Chatterbox); textured cardstocks (Bazzill); letter stamps (Ma Vinci's Reliquary, PSX Design); chalk ink (Clearsnap, Tsukineko); stamping ink; ribbon*

1 Begin by selecting white cardstock with a textured finish. Dab letter stamps lightly with different colored chalk inks. (Heavily inked stamps will cover the cardstock's texture.) Press stamps on cardstock lightly, allowing the cardstock's pattern to show through.

2 Continue stamping, alternating ink colors and letters, until the entire surface is covered.

Mixing Patterned Papers

Mixing patterns can be a challenge. Which floral is best with a stripe? Is there a right-sized gingham to mix with a polka dot? What role does color play in mixing patterns? There are few absolutes when it comes to combining patterns, but following certain guidelines will ensure more pleasing pages. The most important tip in creating successful mixes is to experiment. Pick any sheet of patterned paper from your collection and lay it next to other papers to see what looks best. Mix a white-based design and a cream-based design and see what happens. Place a soft script pattern over a bold geometric one to see what the combination looks like with a small portion of the bold pattern showing. These experiments will better show you how patterns work together (or don't) and will train your eye to see more successful combinations.

David & Jennie
COMBINE FLORALS AND STRIPES

For a page about her brother's wedding, Michelle wanted to create a true shabby look. She chose floral and striped patterned paper from two different companies. She painted and distressed tags and paper to further communicate the look.

Michelle Minken, Memory Makers

Supplies: *Patterned papers (Anna Griffin, K & Company); photo corners (Canson); wooden letter (Walnut Hallow); bottle cap (Manto Fev); eyelets (Creative Impressions); round concho (Scrapworks); definition sheets, microscope slides and letter cut-outs (Foofala); acrylic paint; stamping ink; sandpaper; lace; silver heart charm; hat pin; ribbon; jute; transparency; staples; merchandise tags*

COMMON BASE COLOR

All three patterned papers contain a white base color that meshes them together despite their varying designs and colors.

Kari Hansen,
Memory Makers magazine

Supplies: *Patterned paper (Colorbök, KI Memories, Sonburn); sticker (Pebbles); stamping ink; cardstock; ribbon; hole punch; foam tape*

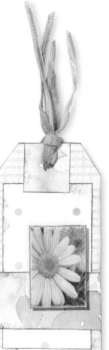

GEOMETRIC & ORGANIC LINES

The difference between the deliberate, repetitive lines of the stripes and the natural, curving shapes of the floral offers a pleasing contrast. The matching greens in each pattern also help them go together well.

Leah Blanco Williams,
Rochester, New York

Supplies: *Patterned paper (Anna Griffin, Provo Craft); Chinese coins (Boxer Scrapbook Productions); stamp (Bunch of Fun); watermark ink (Tsukineko); jute*

TECHNIQUES

USING SOLIDS

The solid black lines effectively separate three different patterned papers that otherwise might blend together.

Leah Blanco Williams,
Rochester, New York

Supplies: *Patterned paper (Kopp Design); ribbon (Offray); textured cardstock (Bazzill); butterfly die cut (Paper House Productions); sentiment sticker (PSX Design)*

SCALE

The variation in scale between these three patterned papers offsets one another. The large polka-dot pattern is dominant. The medium check and small dot patterns do not overwhelm the eye because they are used in smaller amounts.

Kari Hansen,
Memory Makers magazine

Supplies: *Patterned papers (Making Memories); coffee stamp (Wordsworth); ribbon (Offray); stamping ink; cardstock; hole punch; foam tape*

Adding Texture

No matter how you crumple it, there's no doubt that textured looks are hot and add interest to your page designs. While many companies manufacture flat papers with a textured look, it's still fun and so easy to create your own. And the fact that homemade textured paper never turns out exactly the same way twice is just part of the adventure.

Everyone loves Grandma's beach cabin in Manitoba. The screened porch is our favorite place to relax. I caught a very active Lukas in a rare moment of quiet in the afternoon sunlight.   2 years old 2000

Lukas

CREATE TEXTURED BACKGROUND STRIPS

To help emphasize a single photo, Pam mounted a double-matted photo over textured background strips (see p. 121). Crimped title letters and a photo mat add additional elements of texture to this page.

Pam Klassen, Reedley, California

Supplies: *Patterned papers (Bo-Bunny Press, Karen Foster Design, Provo Craft); lettering template (Cut-It-Up); crimpers (Fiskars, Paper Adventures); stamping ink; cardstock*

TECHNIQUES

1 Dab petal ink pads over cream cardstock. Spray cardstock lightly with water to soften paper and blend the ink.

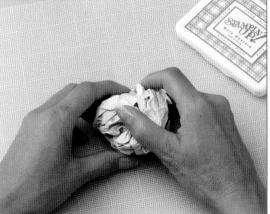

2 While paper is still damp, crumple it into a ball with the ink side in.

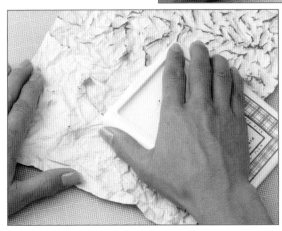

3 Flatten cardstock. Press a rust colored ink pad over the entire sheet.

Distressing

Like your favorite pair of old blue jeans, distressed looks give your scrapbook pages a soft, comfortable feel. Distressing techniques are a great match for both heritage pages and contemporary designs. You can achieve somewhat different results whether you distress with chalk, walnut ink, watercolor paints or other mediums, but all produce the worn, cozy look you're going for.

Connie's Bubby
CRUMPLE AND PRESS TO DISTRESS

This heritage children's portrait inspired Kari to use classic children's illustrations that she printed from a CD-ROM. She distressed each image (see p. 123) and double matted them on ivory and green cardstocks to accent the bottom of the page.

Kari Hansen, Memory Makers magazine

Supplies: *Patterned papers (K & Company, Making Memories, Provo Craft); vintage illustrations (Vintage Workshop); buttons (Magic Scraps); stamping ink; ribbon; thread; cardstock*

CRUMPLING AND IRONING

Give papers a well-used appearance by applying a little distress. Mist paper with water and gently crumple into a ball. Carefully smooth out the paper and air dry. When dry, iron the paper flat using a press-cloth to avoid burning the paper. Emphasize wrinkles and creases by adding touches of stamping ink.

WATERCOLOR TINTING

Reminiscent of the values found in hand-colored photographs and faded fabrics, images tinted with watercolors can have a worn, old-fashioned appearance. Apply watercolors lightly to the inside of a stamped image with a quality, fine-tipped brush.

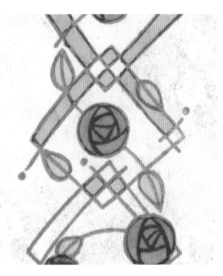

CHALKING

Chalking evokes the look of aged documents, such as browned edges, smudged fingerprints and discoloration and stains. Apply chalk with cotton swabs, make-up applicators or specialty chalking tools to soften the edges of any paper.

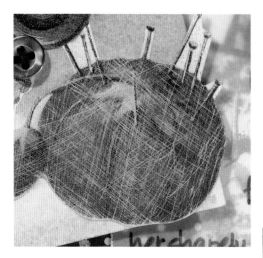

SANDING

The shiny, bright finish of stickers and preprinted accents is easy to tone down with a square of sandpaper. Start with a 220-grit sandpaper, sanding in one direction. If you would like a random cross-hatch design as shown here, first sand in one direction and then in another.

WALNUT INK

Walnut ink provides unique effects in rich browns when applied to paper and fabric. But walnut ink requires a bit of practice, so experiment by painting it in layers on scratch paper first.

What a way to discover natur ride on the Verde Canyon Railro and green colors of the mountai were breathtaking, and the streams and blue skies were endl reminder that going through lif always take the scenic r

VINTAGE STAMPING INKS

As the selection of vintage-inspired stamps has grown, so has the variety of inks to accompany them. A wide range of colors and finishes is available to produce muted, old-fashioned looks. Use vintage ink to define the edges of pages or accents by simply scraping the ink pad around all sides.

Direct-to-Paper Inking

Direct-to-paper inking, long associated with rubber stamping, is a fast and easy technique that adds that little something extra to any scrapbook page. Simply press, pat or swipe an ink pad directly on paper or around the edges—no stamps are necessary.

Absolute Bliss
INK PAPER EDGES

Jenn used direct-to-paper inking to give this layout a vintage look. She applied specially formulated distressing ink around her page background and other paper edges within her layout.

Jenn Brookover, San Antonio, Texas

Supplies: *Patterned papers (Chatterbox, Daisy D's, Design Originals, Li'l Davis Designs, Pebbles, Sweetwater); ribbon (Making Memories, May Arts); wooden flowers (Li'l Davis Designs); page pebble frame (Creative Imaginations); latch (Karen Foster Design); distress inks (Ranger); sandpaper; brads*

Stamping and Embossing

Stamping is a great creative addition to scrapbook pages because it allows anyone to be an instant artist simply by pressing an image to paper. And stamps are a good investment because they can be used again and again. If you've never stamped before, follow the steps below and right to learn the basics.

TECHNIQUES

1 You can use almost any wet colorant to ink a stamp; however, the most common colorants are ink pads and brush markers. Before inking, make sure your stamp is clean and dry. When coloring with ink, gently tap the stamp into the pad, or tap the pad directly onto the stamp. Don't grind or rub the stamp on the pad or apply excessive pressure. Some stamp pads have removable sections that make it easy to color individual parts of an image with different colors.

When coloring with brush markers, color directly on the raised surface with the side of a marker to avoid damaging the tip. If using more than one color, start with the lighter colors first, blending in the darker shades. Brush markers containing dye ink dry quickly, so just before you stamp, "huff" on the stamp with a short burst of your breath to re-activate the ink.

To make sure the stamp design is evenly colored, hold the stamp at an angle to see the ink. If you accidentally ink the rubber surrounding the image, remove it with a cotton swab or baby wipe.

2 Once you've applied color, you're ready to stamp. Carefully position your stamp over the paper in the area you wish to stamp. Press the inked stamp straight down onto the paper without rocking or wiggling. Then lift the stamp straight up. The pressure required depends upon the size of the stamp and the amount of detail, so practice first on scratch paper. If your image is blurry, you may be applying too much pressure or rocking the stamp.

When pressing down large stamps, place the palm of one hand on the top of the stamp. Lay the other hand over the first and press straight down. Another method is to lay the stamp image-side-up and apply the paper on top of the stamp, pressing the paper down using a brayer.

If you stamp with dye ink, the image will air dry quickly, but pigment ink requires more drying time. To expedite the drying process, use a heat gun.

3 After stamping, clean your stamp right away to protect your investment and make future projects easier. You can remove most of the ink using alcohol-free baby wipes or paper towels moistened with water or a mild cleanser (ammonia-free and bleach-free). To remove ink that may be stuck in the crevices, use a soft toothbrush or rub the stamp on a moistened pad. Blot stamps dry with a paper towel or dry rag and store them flat, rubber-side-down, in a cool location.

Basic Embossing

Where there is rubber stamping, heat embossing is never far behind. This quick technique allows stamped images to have a smooth, shiny surface and prevents the ink from smearing. With just two supplies—embossing powder and a heat gun—you'll be ready to emboss page accents, titles and even tiny computer-printed type.

Scenic Sedona AZ
STAMP AND EMBOSS A TITLE AND ACCENTS

Michelle used two ink pads for her title letters, overlapping the colors at the center. After stamping the letters onto blue paper, she embossed with clear powder. For the flower images, she used red ink covered with clear embossing powder (see p. 129).

Michelle Pendleton, Surprise, Arizona

Supplies: *Patterned paper (source unknown); flower stamps (Hero Arts); letter stamps (Club Scrap, Making Memories); nailheads (Scrapworks); stamping ink; embossing powder; pen; cardstock*

1 Rub paper with antistatic pad and stamp image with pigment ink.

2 Sprinkle clear embossing powder on top of image and tap off excess.

3 To emboss, heat image with a heat gun until glossy. Hold gun a few inches from image.

As Good As Gold
EMBOSS COMPUTER FONTS

Sheila used her computer to print the title and captions on clear vellum, which allowed her to adhere the captions over her pictures. After printing each journaling block, she embossed them with gold powder (see p. 131).

Sheila Boehmert, Island Lake, Illinois

Supplies: *Metallic paper (Bazzill); patterned vellum (Westrim); ribbon, bows (Offray); tree and ornament stickers (EK Success); embossing powder; foam tape; vellum*

Creating Embossed Lettering

1 Select a computer font with somewhat heavier lines. (Finely detailed fonts are more difficult to emboss.) Print journaling and title on clear vellum. Thinner vellums seem to work better for this technique as do inkjet printers.

2 Sprinkle gold embossing powder over the type immediately after removing it from the printer. The powder will stick to the wet printer ink. Shake off excess.

3 Use a heat gun to apply heat until embossing powder melts to a smooth finish highlighting the text.

Chalking

Chalk can be the perfect solution for giving paper accents a little bit of added dimension. It's easy to apply and produces soft, subtle results. Use it with templates to create unique designs, or alone for finishing touches on any page.

Use a chalk applicator tool (shown), a cotton swab or your finger to rub chalk along the edges of paper for added color.

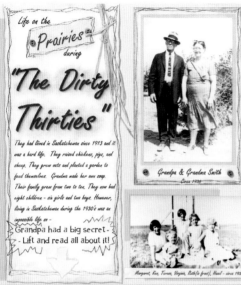

The Dirty Thirties
ADD DIMENSION BY USING CHALK

Sharon's use of muted colors reflects a look appropriate for depression-era photographs. Chalked edges around photo mats and journaling add just a bit of detail to finish the spread.

Sharon Whitehead, Vernon, British Columbia, Canada

Supplies: Fabric-covered wire (Darice); buttons (Hillcreek Designs); chalk (Craf-T); raffia; cardstock; vellum; pens

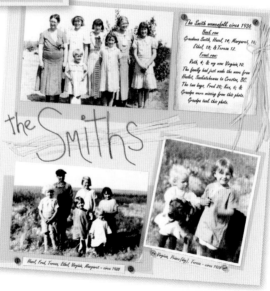

Stitching

The use of both hand- and machine-stitching have become popular in scrapbooking. It can be used as the primary embellishment for pages, but scrapbookers also use it for just a bit of added detail, such as on the corners of a page or a photo mat.

Only You
STITCH A FEMININE PAGE DESIGN

Trudy used stitching and beadwork to create a border that complements the beauty of the little girl in the layout (see p. 135). The use of ribbon, lace trim and a fabric label coordinate with the stitched element.

Trudy Sigurdson, Victoria, British Columbia, Canada
Photo: Kelli Noto, Centennial, Colorado

Supplies: *Mulberry paper (Pulsar Paper); photo corners (Canson); organza bag (source unknown); key (Quest Beads); fabric label (Me & My Big Ideas); textured cardstocks (Bazzill); lace trim; floss; beads; pen; eyelets*

1 To create a floral beaded border, draw a pattern on a paper strip. Temporarily adhere to mulberry strip mounted on pink cardstock strip. Pierce holes through pattern and cardstock to create sewing guide. Remove the pattern.

2 Hand-stitch stems and leaves with green embroidery floss using a backstitch.

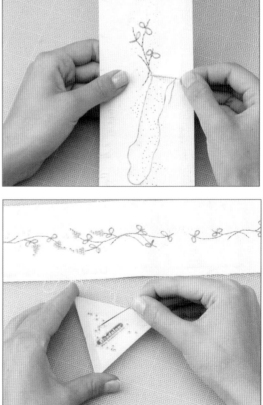

3 Sew pink and white seed beads to the stitched design for embellishment. Add lace trim to the right side and mount on page.

Handcut Titles

Using computer fonts as guides to create handcut titles has revolutionized the art of lettering. With the endless resource of free fonts available online to use as templates, you can always find a lettering style to suit your page theme. While handcutting can be time-consuming and requires the skilled use of a craft knife, there's no other technique that will allow you more customization for titles.

Our Family Tree

CUT OUT APPROPRIATE LETTERS

Stacy downloaded a tree font from the Internet that was a perfect fit for this title block. She printed the word "tree" on beige paper in reverse, then cut around each detailed letter with a craft knife. She then flipped over the letters so the beige color was face-up, adhered them to brown paper and embellished to complete the title.

Stacy McFadden, Park Orchards, Victoria, Australia

Supplies: *Patterned paper, leather pieces, letter stickers (Rusty Pickle); photo turns (Making Memories); cardstock*

My Girlfriends

CREATE SHADOWED LETTERS

Stacy created a shadowed look on this title by cutting out each letter from two different colors of cardstock. She layered the letters onto punched flowers and brown circles for this groovy accent.

Stacy McFadden, Park Orchards, Victoria, Australia

Supplies: *Patterned paper, cut-outs, index tabs (SEI); flower brad (Making Memories); circle and flower punches (Family Treasures); cardstock*

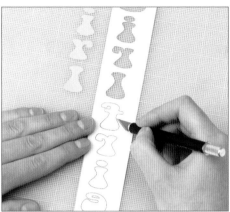

1 Type title and print it twice in reverse on the backsides of green and blue cardstocks. Use a craft knife to cut out letters.

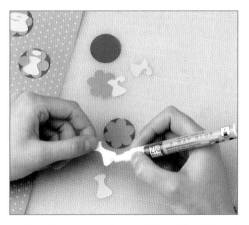

2 Punch and layer shapes. Adhere blue letters to flowers. Layer green letters slightly offset on blue so the "shadow" is visible.

Handmade Embellishments

While there are tons of premade scrapbook embellishments on the market today, it's fun to create your own page accents every once in a while. Doing so will keep you up-to-date on new techniques and help expand your skills. And for unusual page topics, handmade embellishments are often your best bet.

Where the Buffalo Roam
CREATE INTERESTING EMBELLISHMENTS WITH A CRAFT KNIFE

A handcut buffalo accent decorates this Wild West layout (see p. 139). Kelli used the same technique to cut out title words, then created slits for photos in the background paper to further coordinate with the handcut accents.

Kelli Noto, Centennial, Colorado

Supplies: *Cardstocks; pen; foam tape; craft knife*

1 To create the buffalo cut-out, draw or copy the desired image on a separate sheet of paper. Use temporary adhesive to stick the drawn image to the front side of beige cardstock. Cut around the drawn pattern lines with a craft knife. Leave portions uncut for added visual impact and to secure design.

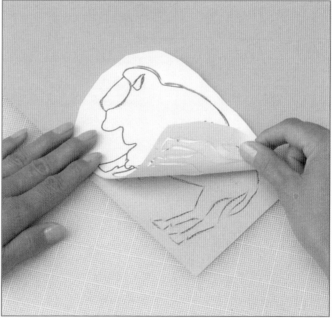

2 Peel off the pattern and remove residual adhesive with adhesive pickup. Mount cut-out over black cardstock with foam tape in between.

Eyelets

Available in every color and a variety of shapes, eyelets are the perfect item for attaching vellum, decorating a photo mat, threading fibers and many other uses. There is a number of tools available to set eyelets, including punches, all-in-one setters, decorative hammers and more. When setting eyelets, just make sure that the hole you punch is not too large and that you use an eyelet setter that fits the eyelet well. Finally, keep in mind that not all eyelets are created equal; some may require more or less pressure to set them depending on the manufacturer.

TECHNIQUES

Little Squirt
USE EYELETS AS DESIGN ELEMENTS

Different sizes of eyelets set all across this page create a lively rhythm appropriate for a little boy learning to use his water gun. A variety of hole punches and eyelet setters was used to correspond to the vast array of eyelets used.

Samantha Walker, Battle Ground, Washington

Supplies: *Eyelets (Making Memories, Prym-Dritz); stamping ink; cardstock; thread*

1 Mark the paper where the eyelet is to be set. Use an anywhere hole punch to make a hole in the designated spot.

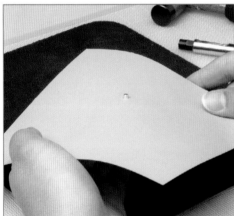

2 Insert the eyelet into the hole.

3 Flip the paper over and place the eyelet setter on top of the eyelet. Pound firmly with a hammer. It may take a few whacks of the hammer to completely set it.

Chapter

Journaling

Journaling is the writing found on scrapbook pages. It can take on many forms, including simple photo captions, lists, poems, essays or stories. While the format varies, the mission is the same: to support your photos and other page elements, and to tell your unique, one-of-a-kind story. The examples in this chapter will show you how to say what needs to be said while adding pizazz to your words. In the end, your pages will include valuable information, while the style in which you write will give the readers of your albums insight into your personality.

Why Journal?

Writing and reading what others have written are the closest things to time travel humanity may ever know. Consider the wonder of it. Perhaps 8,000 years ago a man jotted a note on clay or papyrus. Millennia later the message is found and the thoughts of that long-ago scribe are as clear to you today as they were the day he wrote them.

Like writing, scrapbooking preserves moments in time. You spend time and effort selecting your favorite photos, then carefully designing the best page on which to showcase them. Isn't the story behind those photos worth the same amount of effort? Yes, a picture is worth a thousand words, but those "thousand words" rarely communicate the whole story. Journaling adds context and substance to your scrapbook pages and magnifies the power of your photos. Choose your words carefully, just as you do the photos. The right words will complete the total scrapbooking package for future generations.

To know what information is absolutely essential, think about what those reading your journaling will want to know. Pull out an old photo album or check out a photo-heavy historical book from your library. Cover the captions with your hand and study the pictures. What questions come to mind? Most likely they are the "five W's and the H." That's Who, What, When, Where, Why and How, meaning, who and what are in the photo, when and where was it taken, why did someone want to remember this moment and how did this moment come about? These questions and their answers form the basis of good journaling. Whether you choose to answer them in list form or with poetic verses, use them as guidelines for each scrapbook page.

Uncovering Historical Information

Before you begin to write, you need to know what to write. Facts of past events may have blurred in your memory, or perhaps you're working on a heritage album and never knew the facts to begin with. Consider the following ideas to help.

- *Interview family members and friends about certain memories (see p. 145).*

- *Look in family Bibles in which dates of weddings, births and deaths may be noted.*

- *Read old family letters and diaries.*

- *Visit cemeteries in which family members were buried.*

- *Search newspapers for references to family members.*

- *Find school yearbooks. If you don't have a copy, contact the school.*

- *Ferret out family papers such as wedding and death certificates, mortgage papers, port folios, military commendations, household accounts, receipts, income tax statements and driver's licenses.*

- *Use U.S. census information. Pick up a genealogy book in order to find out how to access it. Search county courthouse records for information about weddings, divorces, property records, wills and deeds.*

Interviewing

Helping others open up about past memories can be a challenge, but you can get the ball rolling on difficult topics by conducting an interview. Good interviewers never ask questions that can be answered with a simple "yes" or "no." Instead, ask leading questions that begin with words such as "why" and "how." (For example: Why did you decide to move to Texas? How did you feel about the move?) While conducting the interview, focus your attention on your subject. Respond to answers by nodding, adding verbal affirmations, and laughing if something is funny. Be sure to give your subject adequate time to reply. Keep note taking to a minimum, writing down "memory joggers" and facts such as dates and names. Better yet, ask if you could tape record the session. Be considerate of your subject by keeping the interview within a time frame that is comfortable to him or her.

Questions to Get Your Subject Talking

- *What is your favorite song or poem and why?*

- *How did your family celebrate holidays?*

- *How would you describe yourself?*

- *How would you like others to describe you?*

- *If you could talk to your descendants 100 years from now, what would you tell them?*

- *Of what are you most proud and why?*

- *What life choice would you change if you knew then what you know now?*

- *What have been the happiest and saddest events in your life?*

- *If you could spend the evening with one famous person—past or present—who would it be and why would you choose him or her?*

Acrostic Journaling

For scrapbookers, a single word can serve as a jumping-off point for more journaling inspiration. The result is known as acrostic journaling. Begin by selecting a single word such as the subject's name or a word that describes him or her. Then write short phrases or sentences beginning with each letter of the word. The sentences should give more detail about the subject. This technique makes it easier to write about someone when those first letters are there to help you get started.

Bloom

OFFER ADVICE THROUGH ACROSTIC JOURNALING

Kimberly chose the word "bloom" to describe the growth of a young child, then came up with advice using each letter in the word as a starting point. She kept the advice short but focused to leave room for other page elements.

Kimberly Kesti, Phoenix, Arizona

Supplies: *Patterned paper (Li'l Davis Designs); textured cardstocks (Bazzill); flower greeting card (Hallmark); mesh (Magenta); letter stamps (Memory Lane); clock hand (Ink It!); stamping ink; cardstock; ribbon; transparency; brad*

Bullet Points

There are no hard and fast rules about how your journaling should be structured. So forget all those old edicts that say you must write in full sentences and have tidy paragraphs. Bullet-point journaling is a perfect, simple option for packing a lot of information into a small space. And because you don't have to write complete sentences, it's less intimidating for a non-journaler to begin.

NY Memories
ADD JOURNALING IN BULLETED LISTS

Amanda summarized an entire trip to New York on a single page by using bulleted lists of journaling. She used different fonts throughout to turn the information into a design element.

Amanda Goodwin, Munroe Falls, Ohio

Supplies: *Patterned paper (Far and Away); cardstock; transparency; brads*

Calendar

Do you scribble notes on the family calendar? The things you jot down reveal important details about the activities in which you and your family are involved. It's where you record both frequent happenings as well as once-a-year milestones. When you journal calendar-style, you have a ready-made basis for getting in all the important details, and your old calendar can serve as a guide.

Cropping Cruise

FORMAT YOUR JOURNALING IN A CALENDAR

Vacation pages are a great place to use calendar-style journaling. Pamela used calendar software to format journaling about the events on a cruise she took.

Pamela James, Ventura, California

Supplies: Calendar Wizard template (Microsoft); cardstock

Classified Ad

Wanted: an innovative way to journal. If that's on your wish list, then classified ad journaling may be just what you're looking for. It's easy, no experience
is necessary and the benefits are exceptional. Simply study the real classifieds
for inspiration and model your journaling after the style, complete with all the
appropriate lingo. It's a great way to add humor to your album or just convey
information in an original format.

Poki
"ADVERTISE" ENDEARING QUALITIES

Stephanie cleverly described her new puppy by writing about all his quirks in a classified ad format.
A copy of real newspaper classifieds creates a fitting backdrop for her title and journaling.

Stephanie Milner, Ventura, California

Supplies: *Metal phrase eyelets, letter charms (Making Memories); silver leafing pen (Krylon); newspaper; cardstock; paper clip*

Comic Strip

Did you hear the one about the scrapbooker who used comic strip journaling in her album? She captured funny dialogue, youthful hijinks and travel misadventures in a panel format, and you can too. It's a fun way to journal that will keep your "audience" laughing and reading until the punch line. Look through your photos with this idea in mind, and you might discover a perfect fit.

The Sunday Funnies
ADD COMIC DIALOGUE

Rachel silhouette-cropped several photos of her son and added "clouds" of comic journaling to fill the open spaces. She designed the page like the Sunday funnies to correspond with the journaling.

Rachel Smith, Vancouver, British Columbia, Canada

Supplies: *Cardstock*

Correspondence

What would you say if you could speak directly to future generations? What truths would you share? What stories would you tell? With correspondence journaling, you have the opportunity to introduce yourself to those you may never meet. In addition, you can record your thoughts for those who might not yet understand to read when they are older. Write a letter to someone and post it in your scrapbook to capture your feelings at a certain time.

JOURNALING

Katie

WRITE A LETTER

Correspondence journaling is a good way to record your thoughts for a child to read when he or she gets older. LeAnn dressed up this letter by changing the font color in certain places and adding brads around the edges.

LeAnn Fane, Powder Springs, Georgia

Supplies: *Patterned paper, metal word charm (K & Company); foam stamps, metal-rimmed tag (Making Memories); number stamp, vellum (Stampin' Up!); fibers (Fibers By The Yard); epoxy heart sticker (Creative Imaginations); cardstock; stamping ink; acrylic paint; eyelet; brads*

Dictionary

The well-known dictionary format provides an easy way to structure your thoughts on a page. Use it to define the qualities you admire in a person or describe a scene in the literal sense. You could copy definitions straight from the dictionary or make up your own for a creative and humorous twist. Inspiration is as close as your local library's reference section!

Beach
USE A DEFINITION

Angelia captured her daughter's blissful disposition and spirit by journaling definitions onto her layout. She used a pink frame to add extra emphasis to the word "happy." Any emotion, sentiment, characteristic or attribute of an event or memory can be expressed easily and succinctly on a scrapbook page by employing this technique.

Angelia Wigginton, Belmont, Mississippi

Supplies: *Patterned paper, label-tape stickers, rub-on letters (K & Company); metal letters, definition sticker, label holder, buttons (Making Memories); brads (Lasting Impressions); rickrack; silk flower; cardstock*

Erasure

Erasure journaling is a pop-art technique used to create artistic sentiments on pages. It is essentially text that is altered to read differently from the way it was originally intended. To employ this technique you'll need a page from a book, magazine, travel guide, junk mail, letter or even an Internet printout. Then apply a variety of mediums over the words to create the effect, including inks and paints along with rubber cement or removable artist's tape. The result is a unique way to add journaling to pages that will also appeal to your artistic side.

A Mother's Love . . .
ALTER PRINTED TYPE

Andrea created erasure journaling for the background of this page using a page torn from a 104-year-old novel. She applied rubber cement over chosen words on the page and allowed it to dry. Next, she added stamped words, ink and paint over the book page. Andrea then rubbed the rubber cement away to reveal words underneath the color.

Andrea Lyn Vetten-Marley, Aurora, Colorado

Supplies: *Patterned paper (Anna Griffin); paper flower, ribbon charms (Making Memories); ribbon (Offray); heart stamp (Hero Arts); dimensional paint (Delta); watch crystal (Magic Scraps); suede paper (Hot Off The Press); metal frames, photo corners, tags (K & Company); letter stickers (Chatterbox); crystal lacquer (Sakura Hobby Craft); watermark ink (Tsukineko); lock and key charms (Boutique Trims); cardstock; measuring tape; fabric; floss; thread; acrylic paint; crayons; heart and cross charms; extra thick embossing powder; fibers; rickrack*

Fairy Tale

Once upon a time there was a scrapbooker who wanted to add something special to her page. Having misplaced her wand, she reached for her computer instead and transformed her writing into a charming story with fairy tale journaling. You, too, can add magic to your pages by adopting a storytelling voice—simply study children's fairy tales and structure your journaling in a similar way. It will bring excitement to any paragraph, assuring that future generations will read it happily ever after.

JOURNALING

Fractured Fairy Tales
JOURNAL FAIRY TALE STYLE

Tricia wrote a modern-day fairy tale using the subjects of her photos as characters. She chose medieval-style fonts to complement the storytelling theme. A gold frame, glass marbles and colorful beads add a decorative touch to the whimsical layout.

Tricia Rubens, Castle Rock, Colorado

Supplies: *Patterned paper (SEI); letter stickers (Doodlebug Design); swirl stamps (Stampin' Up!); gold leafing pen (Krylon); tiny glass marbles (Art Accents); decorative glass beads (JewelCraft); gold frame (Nunn Design); clear plastic tile (Making Memories); cardstock; buttons; wire*

Favorite Things

Chronicling the favorite things of a certain age offers insight into a subject's personality, whether it's your child at age 3 or yourself at 33. Start by choosing categories, then brainstorm lists of favorites to go with each. It's a fun yet organized style of journaling that will allow you to see what was important to a person at a certain time of his or her life.

JOURNALING

Mallory
DOCUMENT THE FAVORITES OF A CERTAIN AGE

Block-patterned paper provided the perfect background for categorizing the favorites of a 2½-year-old. Megan hand wrote the main topic in a larger size, then surrounded each with her daughter's likes, which maximized journaling space.

Megan Jones, Spring, Texas

Supplies: *Patterned papers (Paper Adventures, Paper Illuzionz, Rusty Pickle); metal-rimmed tag, metal letters (Making Memories); letter stickers (Li'l Davis Designs); brads; ribbon; pen*

Found Objects

The written word is everywhere, from brochures and maps to programs and fliers. Take advantage of these printed "found objects" by including them in your scrapbooks and you'll have instant journaling. Such sources can offer added detail when you use them directly on a page or can help you write interesting text of your own.

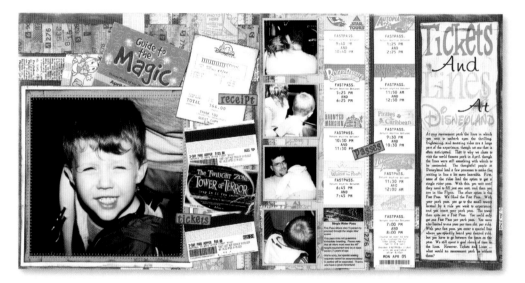

Tickets and Lines
INCLUDE PRINTED MATERIALS FOR JOURNALING

The Disney FastPass tickets on Cherie's page provide added detail about her theme park experience—one filled with tickets and lines. A receipt and brochure include other interesting facts about the trip, which saved Cherie time when journaling.

Cherie Ward, Colorado Springs, Colorado

Supplies: *Patterned papers (Mustard Moon, Rusty Pickle, Sandylion, 7 Gypsies); stamps (Hero Arts); cardstock*

Newspaper Style

Newspaper journalists learn to pack a lot of information into a few short inches. You can do the same on a page when you journal newspaper style. Pick up your local daily for inspiration. Try your hand at writing your own "news" story featuring the most notable people and events in your life. For extra fun, include quotes from the story's major players.

Midland Reporter-Telegram

JOURNAL NEWSPAPER STYLE

Beth created a page to announce her pregnancy showing family members' "reactions." Humorous journaling in a newspaper-style layout make the page special and unique.

Beth Gould, Midland, Texas

Supplies: *Cardstock*

Perspective

Any time you are at a loss for words when it comes to journaling, let someone else speak for you. Hand over a pen and paper to another family member or friend and ask the person to write his or her take on certain events showcased on your pages. You'll receive a fresh point of view that may include details you weren't aware of. In addition, use perspective journaling to give voice to family members who can't speak for themselves, such as family pets.

Always By Your Side
INCLUDE A PET'S PERSPECTIVE

Michelle created humorous and sentimental journaling from the perspective of the family dog for this page. She describes what she believes her dog's feelings for the family would be if he could talk.

Michelle Tardie, Richmond, Virginia

Supplies: *Patterned papers (Daisy D's); fiber (Junkitz); rub-on letters (Making Memories); epoxy letters (Li'l Davis Designs); clear epoxy sticker and number stickers (Creative Imaginations); heart punch, circle punch (Punch Bunch); brads; tag; eyelets; ribbon; cardstock; label holder; acrylic paint*

JOURNALING

When we tire of well-worn ways,
we seek for new.

This restless craving in the souls of men
spurs them to climb,

And to seek the *mountain view*.

-Ella Wheeler-Wilcox

Mountains outside of Pleasant Grove, UT – March 13, 2004

Poetry

When it seems your own words can't quite describe the beauty or excitement of a certain place or event, poetry can help. But you don't have to be Robert Frost to tell a story in verse. Check out poetry collections in books or on the Internet to find something that expresses your feelings. Poetry can enhance the message of the page simply and may even help inspire your page title.

JOURNALING

Mountain View
INCLUDE POETIC VERSE

Becky used the words of a poet to simply enhance a single mountain photo. The words add to the majesty of the mountain without overpowering the photograph.

Becky Thompson, Fruitland, Idaho

Supplies: *Patterned paper (Design Originals); tag (Making Memories); cardstock*

Postcards

Having a wonderful time on vacation? Wish your scrapbook pages were there? Send yourself postcards from the road detailing all the fun (or not-so-fun) events as they unfold. If you visit multiple cities or states on vacation, send cards from each place so you have a record of everything. When you finally return home and are ready to scrapbook about your travels, your journaling will be waiting for you. With the journaling finished, you can concentrate on completing your travel pages quickly.

JOURNALING

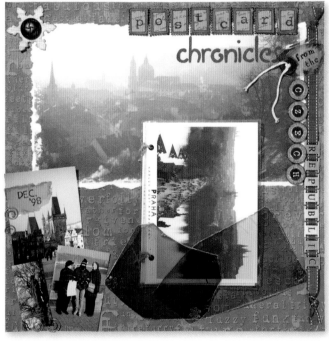

Postcard Chronicles
SEND POSTCARDS TO YOURSELF

On a trip to the Czech Republic, Heidi sent postcards to herself from various locations. She tucked the postcards into a mica pocket on the page, allowing them to serve as a design element as well as journaling information.

Heidi Schueller, Waukesha, Wisconsin

Supplies: *Patterned paper, tag letters (Deluxe Designs); lettering template (Wordsworth); mica (USArtQuest); snowflake brads (Jo-Ann Stores); paper clay (Creative Paperclay Company); letter stamps (Hero Arts, PSX Design); metal letter ribbon charms (DieCuts with a View); letter stickers (EK Success); acrylic paint; cork; stamping ink; eyelets; button; fibers*

Rebus

Sometimes a picture's worth a thousand words, and sometimes it's worth just one. With rebus journaling, you use pictures in place of words. Construct your journaling leaving open spaces throughout to insert images. Add small photographs, stickers, stamps, punches, doodles or anything you can think of that can visually represent what you are trying to say.

A Boy & His Grandpa
ADD PICTURES IN PLACE OF WORDS

Kari used a variety of leftover stickers to journal rebus style. She left out certain words throughout her journaling and spaced the lines far apart to make room for the stickers.

Kari Hansen, Memory Makers magazine

Supplies: Patterned papers (Frances Meyer, Paper Adventures); tags (DMD); letter stickers, paper yarn **(Making Memories)**; stickers (Colorbök, Creative Imaginations, Frances Meyer, Mrs. Grossman's, Paper House Productions, **PSX** Design); cardstock; vellum; eyelets; nailheads; chalk; mulberry paper; photo corners; jute; foam tape

JOURNALING

Recipe

Scrapbooks are a great place to preserve family recipes, but recipe-inspired journaling is more than just a cookbook of culinary favorites. Use recipe journaling to list "ingredients" that make something, or somebody, special. With a teaspoon of imagination, a pinch of inspiration, some photos and a pen, you can whip up an appetizing recipe page.

100% Boy
LIST INGREDIENTS FOR A PERSONALIZED RECIPE

Torrey came up with the perfect "recipe" for a page that pokes fun at what little boys are made of. She journaled on cardstock cut to look like an actual recipe card.

Torrey Scott, Thornton, Colorado

Supplies: *Die-cut letters and lady bugs (Sizzix); cardstock*

Secret Message

Pulling hidden meaning from your journaling can be fun and will appeal to both the artist and the writer in you. The hidden meaning, or secret message written, involves embedding a single word or short phrase into a longer paragraph. Each letter or word is part of different sentences in your journaling. The letters or words of your message are then designed in a way that sets them apart from the paragraph and reveals a special message.

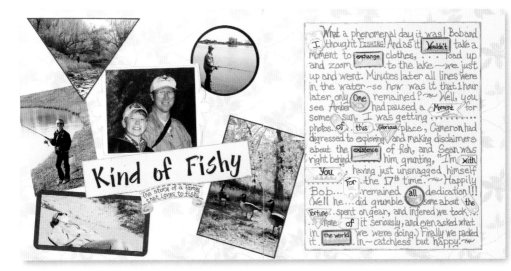

Kind of Fishy
CREATE A HIDDEN MESSAGE

The secret message in Pennie's journaling reads "I wouldn't exchange one moment of this glorious existence with you for all the fortune of the world." Pennie planned the hidden sentence first, then came up with journaling to write around it.

Pennie Stutzman, Broomfield, Colorado

Supplies: *Patterned paper (EK Success); metal-rimmed tags (Making Memories); other tags (DMD); stickers (EK Success, Mrs. Grossman's); metallic rub-ons (Craf-T); pens; cardstock*

Step-by-Step

Many instructional manuals aren't necessarily fun to read, but who wouldn't pore over a how-to pamphlet for putting together a memorable life experience? Step-by-step journaling is a fun way to break down the steps of any activity. It livens up your albums and acknowledges each element that contributes to making a memorable experience.

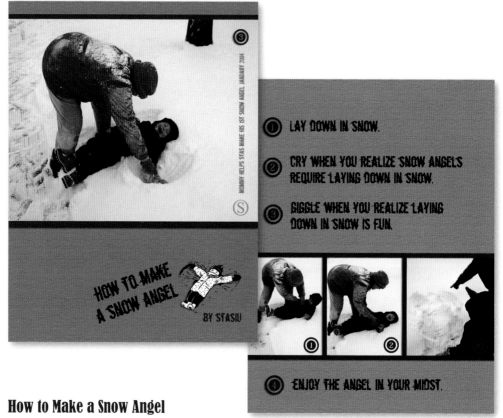

How to Make a Snow Angel
JOURNAL IN STEPS

Ann documented the making of her son's first snow angel by journaling in a step-by-step format. A series of photos complement the journaling style.

Ann Hetzel Gunkel, Chicago, Illinois
Photos: David Gunkel, Chicago, Illinois

Supplies: *Image-editing software (Adobe Photoshop); clip art (www.havanastreet.com)*

Timeline

Capturing all the details from a long span of time can be difficult on a single page, depending on how much time your photographs cover. Timeline journaling can summarize time in an interesting way. Use it to document everything from the minute-by-minute discoveries of a young child to the events of a 50-year marriage.

Moments of Discovery
CAPTURE MINUTES IN TIME

Jodi employed timeline journaling to chronicle her little one's activities as he explored the outdoors. Colored circles house the minutes and add detail to the page.

Jodi Heinen, Sartell, Minnesota
Photos: Caty Kuchinski, Holdingford, Minnesota

Supplies: *Patterned paper (Daisy D's); textured cardstocks (Bazzill); rub-on words (Marking Memories); circle punch (Carl); brads*

Top-Ten List

List-making is easy—you do it every day before grocery shopping or doing chores around the house. This makes top-ten journaling an easy transition. It can help you order and prioritize your thoughts, and just like a grocery list, the order in which they appear doesn't matter as much as the content. Use this style for any number of themes, from love to vacation activities.

10 Things I Love About You
LIST YOUR FAVORITES

On a Valentine's Day spread, Summer recorded the top ten reasons why she loves her husband. Each reason was printed on cardstock, torn out and stitched to the page.

Summer Ford, Bulverde, Texas

Supplies: *Patterned papers (Paper Company, 7 Gypsies); number stamps (Stampin' Up!); letter stamps (Hero Arts); metal letters (Making Memories); stamping ink; cardstock; cheesecloth; rickrack; hemp cord; sandpaper*

Turning Point

The moments, choices and people in your life are important to identify because they will help you realize who you are as a person and what you will become. Start journaling about the turning points in your life, and you'll do more than record who you are. You'll give your loved ones the chance to have an inside look at parts of your personality that may not come up in everyday conversation. Look through old photographs to help jog your memory about certain turning points, and remember that both positive and negative experiences are worth documenting.

My Life to Live
JOURNAL ABOUT A LIFE-CHANGING EVENT

An ended relationship was a turning point for Melonie because she started to think about the kind of person she wanted to become. She journaled about what the experience helped her realize about herself.

Melonie Robinson, Merrill, Wisconsin

Supplies: *Patterned paper (K & Company); pressed flowers (Pressed Petals); mulberry paper; cardstock; vellum; brads*

Conquer Writer's Block

Whether you hand write your journaling or type it on the computer, the important thing is that you put the story behind the photos into words. But any scrapbooker who has sat staring at a blank page or empty screen knows that this can be easier said than done. Here are a few ways to unlock your writer's block.

- *Just do it. Sit down and start writing about anything. It will get your mind going and words on the page. Eventually, you'll warm up to the task.*

- *Keep a journal. Journals are perfect for a no-pressure frame of mind. It will help you flesh out ideas and write without worrying what others will think.*

- *Take a break. Sitting and staring at a blank piece of paper or a computer screen may make things worse. Why not take a break to free your mind? Go for a walk. Take a shower. Let your mind wander. Often, ideas come to us when we least expect it, so keep a notebook and pen handy.*

- *Don't be too hard on yourself. In other words, turn off your inner critic. Everyone must begin somewhere, and only practice makes perfect.*

- *Add your personal spin. When you write, be true to your feelings and describe things honestly. Your personal spin on events will make your journaling meaningful.*

Recording Historic Events

Each generation has significant news—good or bad—that becomes a moment in history. Documenting these events not only preserves history but gives insight as to how you personally were affected by them. Use the following tips to scrapbook about current events.

- *Think about information and insights you wish your ancestors had recorded. Wouldn't it be interesting to know what your ancestors thought about the Civil War? Include this type of information in your journaling.*

- *Include where you were, who you were with and what you were doing when you heard about any significant current event.*

- *List the ways events affected you—physically, emotionally and spiritually.*

- *Did the world or everyday life change as a result of a certain event? If so, how?*

- *Save newspapers and magazines that reported on the event. Scan or photograph items that are too big to fit into your album.*

Using Lyrics, Quotes and Sayings

Still having trouble coming up with the perfect words? Sometimes someone else's words work better than your own. Using a favorite quote or lyric on a scrapbook page can convey a sentiment that you cannot express in your own words.

The "right words" simply are those that are meaningful to you or ones that capture the feeling you're looking for. Maybe you would like to include part of a Maya Angelou poem next to a photo of your late mother. Or perhaps a popular 1960s catch phrase such as "The Age of Aquarius" would be a perfect match in your high school book.

Locating quotes, sayings and lyrics is easy and fun. The Internet is an excellent source for finding virtually any set of well-known words or phrases. Just type "song lyrics" into a search engine (such as www.google.com) and you'll find sites that contain the lyrics to thousands of songs. Many sites list works by artist to make searching easier.

If you prefer a more traditional search style, nothing beats browsing the shelves of a bookstore or library. To find era-specific phrases, scour flea markets, used bookstores and vintage magazine stores for blast-from-the-past books and periodicals.

JOURNALING

Journal the Photos You Don't Have

Have you ever noticed gaps in what you photographed? Perhaps your camera batteries died at a key moment or you were too busy talking to relatives to snap a few shots. Don't skip important events in your scrapbooks just because you don't have photos for them. In times like these, words are the best tools you have to preserve a precious memory and capture the moment.

START WITH THE MEMORY

Create a list of details related to a memory. Write down everything you can remember including everything and anything you did, said, thought or felt and everything or everyone who was (or was not) present. Ask yourself: "What are the most important things I want to tell others about this event or person for which I have no photos?" Trust your intuition here. Often the first thoughts that come to mind are the most significant.

In compiling the list, you will begin to sense what details to include in your albums and how to include them. For instance, remembering a conversation cues you to supplement your missing photos with dialogue (in addition to a description).

If you keep a journal, have letters or anything written such as newspaper clippings, go back to cross-check your list with what is already written down. Cross-check, too, by asking others what they remember. (But do your own list first—that keeps you in contact with what is important to you.)

The Big Five

Emma's hunt for wild predators may not have worked as she'd planned, but now she has a funny story to tell on this page. She printed her journaling on orange paper and layered it with a darker shade. She used a postcard to create the title and accented her page with animal charms.

Emma Finlay, Dublin, Ireland

Supplies: *Charms (Boutique Trims); cardstock*

Weave It Together

Once you are satisfied and feel you have remembered as much as possible, it's time to start writing. Here are suggestions to consider as you do so.

- *Write in short, simple sentences. Don't worry about being fancy as you put ideas and words together. Simple is often best.*

- *Don't worry just now about style, grammar or whether your writing is "good enough."*

- *Write as short or as long a piece as you want to—don't feel constrained by the amount of space on the page just yet.*

- *Keep each paragraph you write focused on one person, idea, event, setting or action. Think of each paragraph as a caption that describes a photo. If you want to go on to describe other aspects of the event, start another paragraph.*

- *Include background information. Why did an event take place? What impact did the event have on the people who were there? What particulars about the event, people or setting do you wish to memorialize?*

- *Present portraits of people. There are two kinds: physical and character. Describe a person's physical appearance through his or her height, eye and hair colors, body type, mannerisms and so on. Character portraits reveal more about what's going on inside someone.*

Wrap It Up

With everything written, you can start editing and narrowing down what you have room to use.

- *When you have finished writing your thoughts, edit your paragraphs for spelling, grammar and readability.*

- *Read all your descriptive paragraphs aloud to help determine which parts are repetitive or less interesting. This will help as you edit to fit the space you have.*

- *Commit yourself to writing and using a descriptive paragraph any time you find yourself saying "I wish I had a picture of..." instead of leaving the memory out of your album.*

Sometimes we stop on the stairs to *enjoy life*

Chapter 6

Computer Scrapbooking

The digital age in which we live has brought with it even more options for creative scrapbookers. Now, computer-savvy scrapbookers can alter photographs, download fonts for journaling, create embellishments that look handmade and even design entire scrapbook pages with the help of today's user-friendly software programs. Explore the many fun facets of computer scrapbooking to decide which ones you would like to start incorporating into your albums.

Computer Scrapbooking Essentials

Computer or digital scrapbooking means different things to different people. On a basic level, it's using your computer to help create scrapbook page elements—such as page titles, journaling blocks and to print photos or clip art. But computer scrapbooking can also encompass complete digital page design by layering backgrounds with photos, fonts and custom-made page accents with just the click of a mouse.

To experiment with computer scrapbooking, you'll obviously need a desktop computer with all the essentials—hard drive, monitor, keyboard and mouse—or a laptop computer. Necessary peripherals—any extra equipment you connect to your computer—include a digital camera and/or a scanner and a printer. An ideal system for scrapbooking will be compatible with your preferred software, will have plenty of extra memory for large image files and a CD burner for archiving images and sharing your digital artwork.

The key pieces of hardware commonly used for computer scrapbooking include a hard drive, monitor, keyboard and mouse. This sleek, budget- and user-friendly system is the HP Pavilion Home PC, with an a820n hard drive and an f1903 monitor. To round out the ultimate "digital darkroom" for computer scrapbooking, added peripherals include an HP Photosmart R707 digital camera and an HP Scanjet 4070 Photosmart scanner.

Digital Cameras

The foundation of all great computer-generated scrapbook pages is great photos. The benefits of using a digital camera include the ability to view pictures immediately after taking them (and easily deleting the less desirable ones) and to easily transfer or download images to the computer. Because these images are already in digital format, they're ready for editing, printing, publishing on the Web or copying to a CD. Today's budget- and user-friendly digital cameras come in all shapes and sizes—from 35mm to compact to ultra slimlines—each with their own unique qualities and features.

Shown left to right are Kodak's DX3500, HP's Photosmart R707, Nikon's D100, Konica Minolta's DiMage X50, Fujifilm's FinePix, HP's Photosmart 935, Concord's Eye-Q 5062 AF and Canon's Powershot A70.

Scanners

A scanner can come in handy for inserting non-digital photographs into digital pages, adding document copies to computer pages and creating custom background papers and digital page accents. A scanner also makes it easier to share or e-mail images and artwork.

Two popular, high-quality and versatile home scanners include the Epson Perfection 4870 Photo scanner and the HP Scanjet 4070 Photosmart scanner. Both offer transparency units for scanning positive/negative film and transparencies.

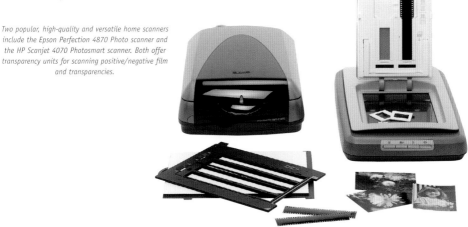

COMPUTER

Printers

The latest computer printers are faster, less expensive and produce better output than their predecessors. Choose a printer that will accommodate the size of photos and digital scrapbook art you wish to print. As a digital scrapbooker, you will want exceptional-quality printed images that will resist fading and yellowing over time.

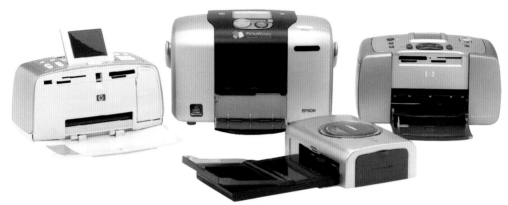

Compact photo printers allow you to print true-to-life photos on the go by inserting the camera card directly into the printer. They're also ideal for printing computer-generated pages for small and mini albums. Shown left to right are the HP Photosmart 375, the Epson PictureMate Personal Photo Lab, the HP Photosmart 245 and the Canon CP-220.

Epson's wide range of printers offers exceptional print quality and excellent longevity at a good price. Featured left to right are the Epson Stylus Photo 960 and the Epson Stylus Photo 1280. The 1280 is great for large-format printing up to 13 x 44", including 12 x 12" digital scrapbook pages.

COMPUTER

Large format printers, like the Epson 2200 printer, can handle media as large as 13 x 44"—great for large scrapbook pages and family tree wall charts. Though this printer is geared more toward advanced amateur photographers and artists, it's a fine choice for digital scrapbooking.

HP offers a wide range of home-use printers perfect for your intended use. Featured left to right are the HP Photosmart 8450, the HP Photosmart 8750 and the HP Photosmart 2610 All-In-One (printer, fax, scanner, copier). These printers offer studio-quality color and superior black-and-white photo printing.

COMPUTER

Printing Papers

Photo-quality papers will give your digital art the look of professionally processed photographs. If your printer supports them, you can print on 4 x 6", 5 x 7" or other precut sizes—including 12 x 12" and even larger when using roll paper and large-format printers. For unique effects, you can also print on cardstock, vellum, canvas and other assorted scrapbooking papers.

Among the top-of-the-line photo papers available are Ilford's Photo Printasia Premium Photo Glossy Paper, Kodak's Glossy Photo Paper, Epson's PremierArt Matte Scrapbook Photo Paper, Janlynn's Cre8's Computer Crafts for Scrapbooking paper, HP's Premium Photo Paper, Epson's Semigloss Scrapbook Photo Paper, Epson's Premium Glossy Photo Paper and Epson's Self-Adhesive Photo Stickers. If you are using photo papers that are not marked "archival quality," protect images with Krylon's Preserve It! The spray helps prevent moisture, fading, early aging, ink runs and damage from smudges.

Software

Purchase an image-editing software program for maximum creative freedom when working with digital photos. Today's image-editing software programs are quite user-friendly. All include basic photographic functions such as rotate, resize, crop, red-eye correction and black-and-white conversion, in addition to special-effect filters and more.

Widely used image-editing software programs include Jasc's Paint Shop Pro 9, Adobe's Photoshop Elements 3.0, Corel's Corel DRAW and Adobe's Photoshop CS (Creative Suite).

More popular image-editing programs include Roxio's Photosuite Platinum 7, Broderbund's The Printshop Deluxe, ACD System's Acdsee7 Powerpack, and ArcSoft's Photo Impression and Photo Studio.

COMPUTER

Image-Editing Tools

Many image-editing software programs contain the same or similar tools; the ones shown here are from Adobe Photoshop Elements CS. The icons may vary from program to program, but the tasks they perform are relatively the same. Getting to know your image-editing software's tools and functions will help make computer scrapbooking quick and easy!

 RECTANGULAR MARQUEE
Use this tool to make a rectangular selection on your image. Hidden tool: Elliptical marquee: Use to make circular and oval selections.

 LASSO
Use to make a freehand selection around a part of your image. Hidden tools: Polygon Lasso and Magnetic Lasso.

 SELECTION BRUSH
Use to brush in area to be selected.

 CUSTOM SHAPE
Rectangle tool: Use to draw a rectangle on the page. Hidden tools include: Line tool: Use to draw lines. Shape selection tool: Use to select shapes of choice.

 PAINT BUCKET
Use to flood an enclosed area of your image with color of choice.

 BRUSH
Use to paint on the image using the foreground color as the paint color.

 ERASER
Use to erase parts of the image. On the background layer, erasing replaces the image with the background color. On a layer, erasing the image removes it completely, allowing other layers below to show through. Hidden tool: Background Eraser: Use to remove the background detail.

 BLUR
Use to blur by dragging over area of image you want blurred.

 SPONGE
Use to subtly change color saturation or vividness of an image area.

 DODGE
Use to add brightness. Effective in adding dimension and shadows.

 CLONE STAMP
Use to retouch an image by copying an area of an image and stamping it over another. Hidden tool: Pattern Stamp: Use to paint with a pattern you select.

 HAND
Use to view another area of the image.

 FOREGROUND COLOR
Click this color to open the Color Picker to choose another color for the foreground.

 BACKGROUND COLOR
Click this color to open the Color Picker to choose another color for the background.

 SWITCH COLORS
Click arrows to switch from foreground to background color and vice versa.

 MOVE
Use to move a layer or the selected area to a new position on the image.

 MAGIC WAND
Use to select areas in the image by selecting areas of similar color.

 CROP
Use to select an area of the image that you want to retain (the area outside this is discarded).

 TYPE
Click to type text onto your image. Press Enter to start a new line. Hidden tools include: Vertical Type tool for creating vertical type.

 GRADIENT
Use to fill an area with a blend of two or more colors of choice.

 PENCIL
Use to draw freehand lines on the image.

 RED-EYE BRUSH
Use to remove red-eye from people and animals in images.

 SHARPEN
Use to increase the clarity of edges in an image.

 **SMUDGE**
Use to smudge colors in an image.

 **BURN**
Use to darken areas of the image, adding shadows and dimension.

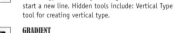 **EYEDROPPER**
Use this to sample colors from your image to use to paint or fill areas, etc. Click the Eyedropper and then hold it over an area of your image and click to select the color under the mouse cursor as the foreground color.

 **ZOOM**
Click to select the tool, then click on the image to zoom in. Hold the Alt key as you click to zoom out.

TOOLS

Designing a Digital Page

Armed with a basic understanding of what computer-generated scrapbooking is as well as some available hardware, software, paper and ink mediums, you're ready to make your first digital scrapbook page. For the purpose of this tutorial, we've used Adobe Photoshop CS. Most image-editing software programs have similar features, but if they are unfamiliar to you, check your software manual or do an on-screen Help search to identify similar tools in your software program.

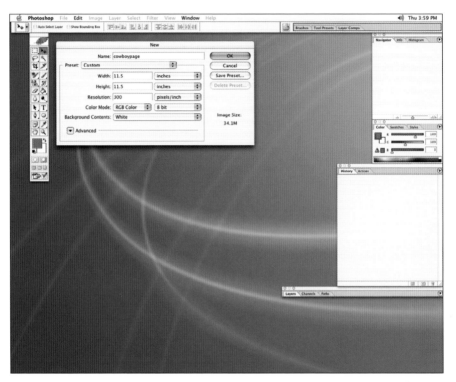

illustration A

Create the Background

1 Launch or open your software to create a page background in the desired size. Choose File, New and select the width and height of your page. Set resolution at 300 pixels/inch. For standard printers, make an 8½ x 11" page. For large-format printers, create an 11½ x 11½" background. Set color mode for RGB color (illustration A).

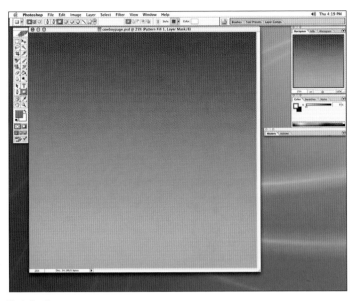

Style the Background

2 To create a solid background, choose a foreground color (in this case, orange; illustration B), then use the Paint Bucket tool to color the background.

illustration B

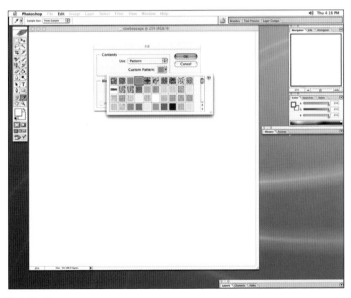

illustration C

To create a patterned background, select Edit, Fill, and from the Use drop-down list, choose Pattern and select a built-in pattern (illustration C).

COMPUTER

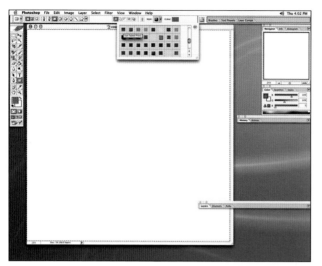

Another option is to click on the Rectangular Marquee to select all, click on rectangular shape, then select a Style from the dropdown list (in this case Sun Faded Photo) and drag it to the background (illustration D).

illustration D

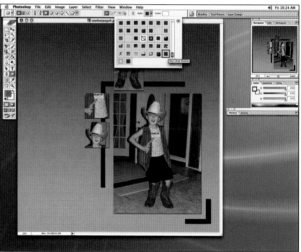

Add the Images

illustration E

3 If you wish to add color blocks or borders to the background first, click on the rectangular Shape tool and drag the pointer across the page with your mouse to draw your shapes. Select a foreground color and use the Paint Bucket tool to fill in the shapes with color (in this case, black). For photos, click File, Open to open the images you want to use on the page. You can go ahead and crop or resize the images first or drag the Rectangular Marquee tool across the part of the images you want to use. Choose Edit, Copy and then Paste the images onto the background. Use the Move tool to position where desired. Finally, use the rectangular shape tool and click on Style to add drop shadows, beveled edges or mats to the photos (illustration E).

Add Title

4 Click on the Text tool. Select a font (in this case, Rosewood Std), font size (in this case, 72) and color (we used black) and then type the title directly on your background (illustration F). Elaborate or fancy fonts work best for page titles. To find a font that goes well with your page theme, highlight your title by drawing your mouse over it and experiment by changing to different fonts for the look you desire. Use the Move tool to position the title where you want it on the page.

illustration F

illustration G

Add Journaling

5 Follow the same steps you used to create the title to add journaling. Select a simple font for the journaling text (we used Cochin at 15-point size; illustration G) to make the journaling easier to read and so it won't compete with the title. Based on your page design or the look you want to achieve, select left-, center- or right-justified text formatting for the journaling (we used left-justified). Use the Return key on the keyboard to experiment with bumping words down a line if needed for visual appeal.

COMPUTER

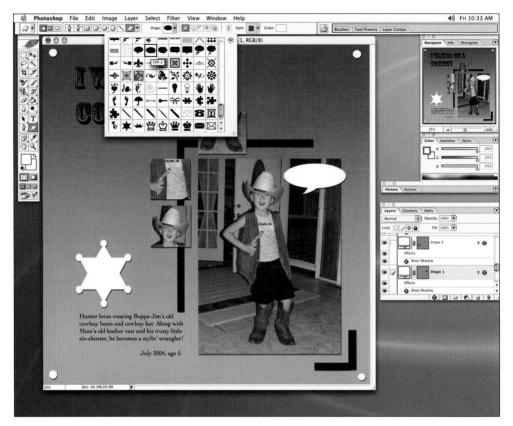

illustration H

Add Page Accent Shapes

6 Use the Shape Marquee tool to select shapes that work well with your page theme. If your software is new, you can use the Append command (the tiny arrow on the dropdown menu will reveal the rest of the shapes by theme) to load all the shapes that came with the software. Click on a shape (in this case, a conversation bubble and sheriff's badge were used; illustration H) and then use your mouse to draw the shape in the desired size directly on the page; use the Move tool to position where desired. Use the Ellipse shape to draw small circles for digital faux brads as seen on the corners of the page.

illustration I

Style Page Accents

7 Click on the Freeform Shape tool to select the shape you wish to style then select a Style from the dropdown menu (in this case, woodgrain; illustration I) to add texture and dimension to the shapes.

Add Text to Page Accents

8 Click on the Text tool and select a font, size and color. Then type directly over page accents to personalize them (illustration J) and use the Move tool to position text where desired.

Isn't it fun? You've just completed your first computer-generated scrapbook page, and with a little experimentation, the sky is the limit to your digital creativity!

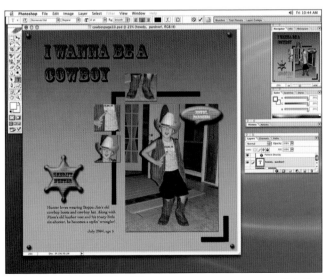

illustration J

Internet Resources

For traditional scrapbookers, there are hundreds of Web sites that can give you a crash course in digital scrapbooking. You'll find tutorials on various techniques, plug-ins and custom brushes to add to your creative repertoire and find ideas for creating your own backgrounds, fibers, page accents and more. You'll also find resourceful chat rooms and message boards for learning, as well as downloadable page elements. Here are just a few:

www.computerscrapbooking.com

www.cottagearts.net

www.digitaldesignessentials.com

www.digitalscrapbookdesign.com

www.digitalscrapbookplace.com

www.escrappers.com

www.esticker.com

www.gauchogirl.com

www.hp.com/scrapbooking

www.littlescrapper.com

www.pagesoftheheart.net

www.printlabseries.com

www.scrapbook-bytes.com

www.scrapbook-elements.com

www.scrapbookgraphics.com

www.scrappersguide.com

www.twopeasinabucket.com

Heaven
DOWNLOAD PAGE ACCENTS

To create this soft and sophisticated baby layout with a handmade appearance, Doris downloaded a variety PagePaks and AlphaSets accents from an Internet site.

Doris Castle, Fonda, New York

Supplies: *Page accents (CottageArts.net); image-editing software*

COMPUTER

Using Digital Downloads

There are many creative things you can do with downloaded digital kits and elements. They can be used as is by simply adding your photos, title and journaling, or you can experiment with changing colors to suit your computer-scrapbooking needs. Use downloaded elements over and over again for a fresh new look every time!

Sweet Nothings
COORDINATE DOWNLOADED ELEMENTS

Tonya's page was created with elements from her custom collection Love Letters, available on the Internet as a free download. The coordinated collection contains patterned papers, embellishments and an alphabet already created in digital format so she could enhance or change it as needed.

Tonya Doughty, Wenatchee, Washington

Supplies: *Downloaded page kit (www.gauchogirl.com/mmsbcomp.htm)*

Creating Digital Papers and Paper Accents

One secret to stunning computer scrapbook pages is the background with which you start. Image-editing and computer-scrapbooking software programs offer an endless array of backgrounds and colors to choose from. By experimenting with gradations, color saturation, opacity, brushes and filters, it's easy to achieve the precise style, pattern and texture you're looking for to help showcase your photographs. Once you're comfortable designing your own "papers," use the same techniques to mimic popular page accents such as tags, slide mounts, library tabs, ribbons, paint chips and more.

. . . Enjoy Life
CHOOSE A SINGLE-COLOR BACKGROUND FOR IMPACT

The black-and-white focal-point photo and colorful accent images on Traci's page stand out when placed on a solid black background. Words in white add impact while keeping the page simple.

Traci Turchin, Hampton, Virginia
Photo: Rice Photography, Lakebay, Washington

Supplies: *Image-editing software (Adobe Photoshop CS)*

Utah's Hogle Zoo
CREATE A POSTAGE STAMP SHEET

Starting with a simple white background, Angela duplicated the look of a postage stamp sheet by using a round brush to draw dotted lines between her photos. To create the virtual wax seal, she experimented with different layer styles including bevel/emboss on a shape. Elements such as the paw-print clip art become dimensional when Angela applied drop shadows or inner shadows to them.

Angela M. Cable, Rock Springs, Wyoming

Supplies: *Image-editing software (Jasc Paint Shop Pro 8); clip art (source unknown)*

The Makings of Peer Pressure
ADD DEPTH TO COLOR BLOCKING

Shannon's clever use of color blocking and digital chalking brings depth and dimension to her art while drawing the eyes straight in to the photos featured. To create diagonal lines, she used the Rectangular Shape tool and varied the opacities of each line. To "chalk" the lines, she used the Spray Paint tool, then applied a Gaussian Blur effect.

Shannon Freeman, Bellingham, Washington

Supplies: *Image-editing software (Micrografx Draw 6.0, Microsoft Photo Editor, Microsoft Paint)*

COMPUTER

Photo Manipulation

One of the most fun yet challenging aspects of computer scrapbooking is photo manipulation. With a click of the mouse you can transform an image into a clever piece of digital photo art. The more familiar you are with your image-editing software, the more enjoyable photo manipulation will be. Take advantage of the software's on-screen help tutorials or user manual while experimenting. Explore the software's features on just one photo, practicing simple things like resizing and cropping images. Then adjust the contrast or hue/saturation levels. With each tool you apply, note how the image is transformed. Undo each adjustment and move on to the next adjustment. When you feel comfortable with basic photo manipulation, begin working in layers. Try adding text to an image and experiment with different artistic effects. Remember that if you don't like a certain effect, you can always undo it. An entire world of photo creativity awaits!

COMPUTER

Aspirations
CROP PHOTOS DIGITALLY

Shannon cropped images from photos so she could change the backgrounds of each. She used the eraser tool to remove the original backgrounds of her subject and a photo of his arm, then added wood and sky images behind them.

Shannon L. Freeman, Bellingham, Washington

Supplies: *Image-editing software (Micrografx Draw 6.0, Microsoft Paint)*

During Spring Break we visited the Anasazi Pueblos which date to 1100-1300 A.D. The preserve was opened in 1907 and it includes one of the rarest collections of cliff-dweller relics in existence. It was so cool; the guys loved it! March 2004

Manitou Cliff Dwellings
APPLY SHAPES TO PHOTOS

MaryJo used pre-designed shapes that came with her page design software to add character to her photos. To expound further on her photos' theme, she used her own hand-drawn clip-art petroglyphs for a custom background.

MaryJo Regier, Memory Makers Books

Supplies: *Page-design software (HP's Creative Scrapbook Assistant); clip art (artist's own design)*

This Is My World
SILHOUETTE CROP A SUBJECT

Angel turned an average shot of her little boy holding a ball into a compelling scrapbook page with a fun message. She masked the background of a photo leaving just the child and the ball, then replaced the background with half black and half blue. The lens flare filter created the stars on the black part of the background. She then masked the ball and replaced it with a clip-art photo of the earth.

Angel Richards, Kennesaw, Georgia

Supplies: *Image-editing software (Adobe Photoshop 7)*

On the joys of raising Little boys. There is not a day that goes by that you are not claiming ownership of something that is not, rightfully yours. But someday, I hope You can have the world.

THIS IS MY WORLD

I AM 2 YEARS OLD

AND YOU CAN'T PLAY WITH IT!

COMPUTER

Having Fun With Fonts

You don't have to be a graphic artist to understand how to work with fonts successfully. There are generally two types of fonts—serif (has little lines or curves resembling pen strokes called serifs at the ends of each character) and sans-serif (doesn't have these embellishments). Serif fonts help the eye move from word to word and are generally easier to read than sans serif fonts. With all the fun and fancy lettering available, classic fonts might seem a little boring, but they do go with anything and are easy to read. With fonts, less is more. Choose appropriate fonts for page titles and journaling, which should contrast with each other in terms of style, size, color or boldness. In other words, don't mix similar fonts. Remember, the main goal with fonts is readability and a polished appearance. Have fun!

A Smile Can Happen
MIX FONTS TASTEFULLY

Dena used various type styles in different hues, sizes and orientations to effectively counterbalance candid shots of her son. When overlapping fonts, she contrasted the colors and opacity so they could be easily read.

Dena Simoneaux, Henderson, Nevada

Supplies: *Image-editing software (Adobe Photoshop CS); custom brushes (www.annikavonholdt.com; www.1greeneye.net)*

Look Up
ROTATE FONTS VERTICALLY

Staggering script fonts with serif fonts in different sizes makes an attractive combination on this page. Ronnie also adjusted the opacity of certain words for additional appeal. She created separate text boxes for each word in image-editing software, which allowed her to rotate the title vertically and position other words exactly where she wanted them.

Ronnie McCray, St. James, Missouri

Supplies: *Image-editing software (Adobe Photoshop Elements 2.0) world clip art (source unknown)*

Turning Twelve
ALTERNATE FONT COLORS

Switching off between black, white and yellow text and rectangular blocks makes Sande's page dynamic. Wrapping the word "Moving" onto the next line adds drama and aids in the block text formation, as does the decreasing font size and the lowercase letters as the words move downward.

Sande Krieger, Salt Lake City, Utah

Supplies: *Image-editing software (Adobe Photoshop 7)*

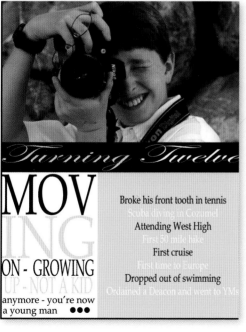

COMPUTER

Creating Digital Embellishments

Similar to traditional scrapbooking, page accents or embellishments are the last touch you'll add to a computer-generated scrapbook page. And these digital page accents are anything but flat. By applying artistic filters, plug-in effects or tool adjustments, two-dimensional page accents will leap from your computer-generated scrapbook page with character, depth, sheen and texture. Experiment with geometric shapes and various effects to create digital renditions of page accents you've grown to know and love from the world of traditional paper scrapbooking.

Of Men and Cars
CREATE DIGITAL BOTTLE CAPS AND NAILHEADS

Retro fonts, vintage colors and chrome give Angela's layout just the right touch of 1950s nostalgia. On a blue background, red, tan and cream starbursts were added using the Preset Shape tool's Star1 shape set with a thin black outline. Angela used the Balls and Bubbles Artistic Effect to create the faux screws, which are enhanced by adding an X with a Cutout 3D Effect. To create the bottle caps, Angela selected the Gear5 Preset Shape tool, then applied a Chrome filter > Bevel > Drop Shadow. Decals on each bottle cap were hand-drawn and fonts were added.

Angela M. Cable, Rock Springs, Wyoming

Supplies: *Image-editing software (Corel Paint Shop Pro 8); plug-in filters (Alien Skin Eye Candy 4000, Flaming Pear Super Blade Pro); automobile logo (source unknown)*

Beach Baby
ADD FAUX BEADS

Small, textured baubles add pop to Angela's digital page. Sandals were created with a hand-drawn shape; Texture effect was then used and a bead was added with Picture Tube effect applied. A second sandal was created by using the Image > Mirror option. To create a string of faux letter beads, Angela made circle shapes in different hues with different levels of Bevel and Drop Shadow 3-D effects. Letters were given an inner bevel to finish.

Angela M. Cable, Rock Springs, Wyoming

Supplies: *Image-editing software (Corel Paint Shop Pro 8)*

Nine Months
DESIGN METALLIC ACCENTS

Faux metal accents are the perfect addition to Kristie's digital grunge page. After creating a ribbon buckle, eyelets and round tags on the computer, Kristie applied the Chrome Effect filter to each to add a shiny metal appearance.

Kristie L., Houston, Texas

Supplies: *Image-editing software (Adobe Photoshop 7); filter (Alien Skin Eye Candy 4000 chrome)*

COMPUTER

Digital Organization and Storage

Computer scrapbookers have the benefit of creating hundreds of photographs and computer scrapbook pages at little or no cost, but this can mean much more to organize and store. Your photos and pages could wind up in various places on your hard drive, making them difficult to locate and taking up valuable memory. A good organizational system is key.

CHOOSE A SOFTWARE STORAGE PROGRAM

There are numerous photo-storage programs available to store and organize your digital images. In fact, most cameras come with some type of software for both storage and editing.

DECIDE WHAT TO KEEP

It is tempting to keep all your photos, but storing bad digital photos will only create frustration when scrapbooking. Delete the bad photos when you download them from your camera. If you'd like to try to fix certain photos with image-editing software, do so before you store them.

CREATE A NAMING SYSTEM

Choose a simple and consistent naming system that you will remember and will allow you to retrieve your photos quickly. Begin by labeling your photos with the year. Next, specify an event and add a topic (example: 2004_xmas_topic.tif). Likewise, store any computer scrapbook pages made with those photos together in the same folder prior to burning the images to CD.

STORAGE OPTIONS

Burning images and art onto CDs is probably the most common method for storing digital photos. It is easy, inexpensive and compact. Store your disks in a way that will prevent scratching. In addition, many online photo-processing companies offer photo storage with password-protected access. While it's always a good idea to have a backup storage system, online storage allows friends and family to view and print your photos from anywhere. Another option is to purchase an extra hard drive just for digital photo storage. This is not completely uncommon with die-hard digital photographers and scrapbookers. It can be very efficient in terms of the limitless number of photographs you can store on it.

COMPUTER

Keep organized with Fellowes' Compact Disc Multi-Media Drawer, CD/DVD Labeling Starter Kit and Maxell Slims CD Cases.

Sharing Digital Artwork

One of the biggest rewards of computer scrapbooking is the joy of sharing the digital art with others. Some scrapbookers print their pages onto archival photo paper, slip them into page protectors and then into scrapbook albums, just like traditional scrapbook pages.

If your desire is to share your computer-generated pages on the Internet, there are a number of ways to do so after you've saved your layouts. When saving your layouts, many scrapbookers prefer to save two versions of the finished pages: a high-resolution version and a low-resolution version. High-resolution layouts, created and saved at 300dpi, will be ready for printing onto photo paper any time you need them. Save a low-resolution version of the original art at 72dpi for viewing on private Web sites, public digital-scrapbooking forums, sending as e-mail attachments and more.

A good number of digital camera and image-editing software packages also include powerful tools for organizing and sharing artwork, creating cards and calendars, sharing images on mobile phones and PDAs, burning CD slide shows for TV viewing and automatic backing-up of photos onto CD.

However you choose to share your computer-generated masterpieces, one thing is certain: They will wow and amaze everyone who sees them!

Smart and simple software that make creating, organizing and sharing computer scrapbook layouts a breeze are Nova Development's Photo Explosion Deluxe and Jasc's Paint Shop Photo Album 5 Deluxe Edition.

Chapter

Workspace Efficiency and Cropping On-The-Go

The social aspect of scrapbooking is as important to some as creating beautiful pages. Scrapbookers are constantly packing up their supplies to crop with friends and attend retreats, so it's important to have supplies that travel easily. In addition, this chapter includes ideas on how to make the most of your time spent with other scrapbookers, as well as tips for starting a group of your own. Your favorite hobby will be even more fulfilling when you collaborate with other creative individuals who share your passion.

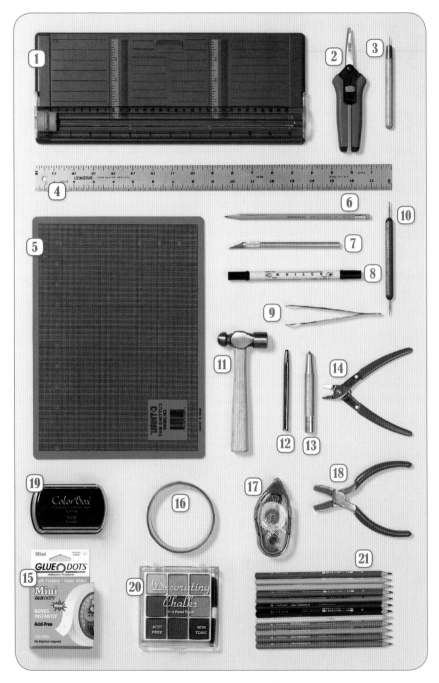

Create a Basic Tool Kit

There are so many tools and gadgets available for scrapbookers, how do you decide what is necessary to buy immediately and what can wait? In the most basic sense, beginners should purchase a quality black pen for journaling, a paper trimmer for cropping photos, adhesive, cardstock for backgrounds and an album. From there, the tools and supplies you add can reflect your personal style and the looks you enjoy creating. For example, if you love to use eyelets, a hammer and eyelet setting tool would be high on your priority list. If stamping is your thing, you'll need ink, stamps, embossing powder and a heat gun. Maybe you are too new to scrapbooking to really know what techniques you like best. Consider taking a few scrapbooking classes on a variety of topics from a local store.

Below is a list of tools most frequently requested or considered necessary to bring to classes. Build an all-around basic tool kit from this list. Keep the items together so they are easy to toss in your crop bag and take with you. You could also use this list to create a gift basket for a beginning scrapbooker.

1. paper trimmer
2. scissors
3. paper piercer
4. straightedge ruler
5. cutting mat
6. pencil
7. craft knife
8. archival black pen
9. tweezers
10. stylus
11. hammer
12. hole punch
13. eyelet setter
14. wire cutters
15. adhesive dots
16. heavy-duty double-sided tape
17. adhesive runner
18. jaw pliers
19. black ink pad
20. chalk
21. colored pencils

Pack a Page Kit

Creating your own custom page kits will save time when you sit down to scrapbook, especially if you leave home to crop. You'll have all your photos, paper and embellishments directly in front of you to make a specific page. As you get your photos developed and choose the ones you'd like to use for pages, gather coordinating paper and embellishments that complement the photos. When you go to a crop, just grab a couple of pre-bagged projects and your travel scrapbook kit. This saves time when packing and helps you concentrate on the project at hand.

1 Gather photos for a specific page and make journaling notes. Stick them to the backs of the corresponding photos.

2 Choose coordinating paper for backgrounds and mats. Select embellishments that complement the theme.

3 Pack all supplies in a plastic project folder, and label it.

CROP ON-THE-GO

On-The-Go Storage Solutions

If you usually leave your home to scrapbook, you will need a portable storage unit. While there are many such products on the market specifically designed to hold scrapbooking supplies, general art supply storage products are also useful.

Customized options for on-the-go scrapbookers range from backpacks and shoulder bags to cases on wheels and plastic storage totes. Many of these carryalls have designated compartments and pockets for safely storing tools and supplies—such as punches, stamps, decorative scissors and pens. Many have special compartments for toting 12 x 12" and 8½ x 11" papers and sturdy compartments for storing heavy 12 x 12" albums. Add a luggage identification tag with your contact information, and your tote will be ready to take anywhere.

Crop In Style's Paper Takers store paper neatly and safely and are available in 12 x 12" and 8½ x 11".

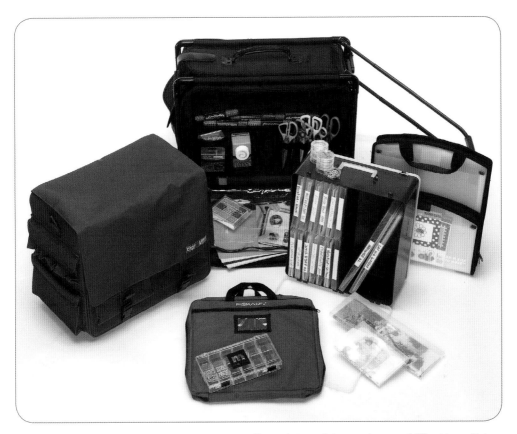

Most product manufacturers produce several different types of totes and carryalls for scrapbooking on-the-go. From backpacks and shoulder bags to handled totes on wheels—you're sure to find exactly what you need to suit your scrapbooking style.

Personalize Your Crop Bag

You roll your bag into a crowded cropping room, convention hall or class to find a sea of carriers that are identical to yours. Don't let your bag get lost in a crowd—personalize it! Decorating a crop bag to suit your personal style can be fun and will help you feel right at home. Who knows, it might just inspire a page design and motivate you to stay organized. Once your bag is decorated, take it a step further by embellishing your supplies a little. No one will accidentally walk away with your favorite pen or scissors if you've truly made them your own with decorative accents. You'll take home everything you came with and be the talk of the crop with such stylish supplies.

1 Tear strips of fabric in your favorite colors and tie them to your bag to quickly identify it in a crowd.

2 Label ink pads with bright, easy-to-spot acrylic paint so there is no mix up with someone else's inks.

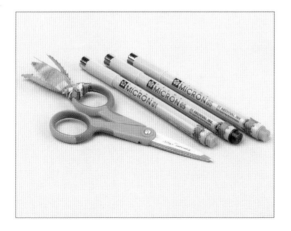

3 Everyone will know to whom these scissors and pens belong when you tie on colorful fabric swatches that coordinate with your crop bag.

CROP ON-THE-GO

Scrapbook Ergonomics

We've all heard of tennis elbow, but what about cropper's elbow? Or cropper's neck, back, hands and eyes, for that matter? If you've spent even a few hours cropping, you've no doubt endured crop-related pain. That pain can slow you down, or worse, develop into a chronic injury.

Croppers are susceptible to several injuries that can affect the hands, wrists and back. Incorrect posture and repetitive and forceful tasks cause tendons, muscles and nerve tissue excessive wear and tear.

Croppers typically practice risky postures while crafting: hunched shoulders; bent/flexed wrists; repetitive hand, arm and shoulder motions; long reaches for materials; long periods of sitting and on nonadjustable chairs; working with the neck bent and using pinched grips on pens, pencils and cutting tools.

The good news is that simple changes in your posture and workspace or workstation setup will make noticeable differences and lead to healthier habits surrounding your hobby.

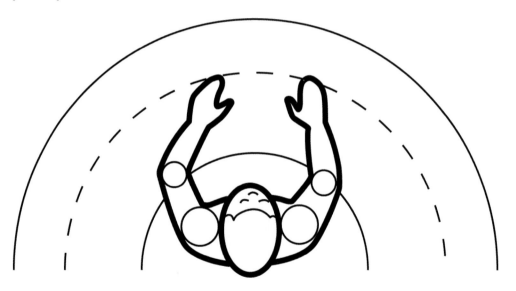

Easy Reach Zone

Keep supplies around you in a semicircle—within the Easy Reach Zone. This will keep you from repeatedly straining to reach certain tools and risk injuring yourself over time. Supplies used most frequently should be the closest to you; supplies seldom used should be farthest. Organize tools and supplies from left to right, or right to left, in the order in which you use them.

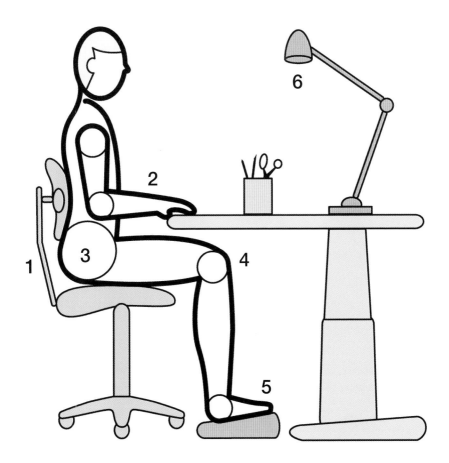

This is an ergonomically correct cropper. Take note of the following:

1. *The lumbar area, or lower back, is supported, and the cropper exhibits neutral back, shoulder and neck posture.*

2. *The crop station is at forearm level to keep wrists straight and neutral.*

3. *The hips are slightly higher than the knees.*

4. *The knees are bent at a 90-degree angle.*

5. *Feet are flat and a footrest is utilized to compensate for short stature.*

6. *Task lighting exists to reduce eyestrain.*

CROP ON-THE-GO

Ten Tips for Healthier Scrapbooking

Follow these suggestions to help avoid the pains
and strains that long periods of cropping can cause.

1. *Vary tasks and take breaks to increase productivity. Set a timer to remind you to take short breaks.*

2. *Incorporate simple stretches and exercises into your crops. Build up muscle groups that feel the effects of scrapbooking, like the shoulders and hands.*

3. *Use tools that decrease force whenever possible.*

4. *Support the lower back with a lumbar pillow or rolled-up towel.*

5. *Use a footrest or phone book to help keep knees at a 90-degree angle.*

6. *Increase task lighting to alleviate eyestrain.*

7. *Use different workstations for different tasks. Use sitting stations for precise work, such as beading, and standing stations for force-intensive work, such as punching or stamping, to permit more efficient use of the upper body.*

8. *Keep often-used tools and supplies within the "swing space," or within the Easy Reach Zone (see p. 208).*

9. *Orient your work to suit you whenever possible. Redesign the task to keep your body in a neutral position.*

10. *Work at forearm level to keep arms, neck and shoulders relaxed and wrists straight and neutral.*

8 Ergonomic Scrapbooking Products

1. TUTTO BAG

Tylenol and the Arthritis Foundation bestowed a design award on this bag for being back-friendly. It's easy to pull and maneuver, and it's versatile and durable. (tutto.com)

2. FOOTREST

Shorter croppers can keep their feet flat with a footrest, such as this one from McGill, Inc. (mcgillinc.com)

3. PENCIL/KNIFE GRIPS

Grips increase the contact area on narrow tools, such as pens and craft knives. These are from The Pencil Grip. (thepencilgrip.com)

4. LUMBAR PILLOW

Strap this lumbar pillow to a chair to support the lower back. Check back stores and the Internet for one that suits you.

5. DAYLIGHT TASK LIGHT

Proper light reduces eyestrain and promotes good posture. It also eliminates glare and shadows. (daylightcompany.com)

6. STRONGARM PUNCH

The Strongarm from McGill reduces the amount of force needed to punch. (mcgillinc.com)

7. FISKARS SCISSORS

Soft Touch scissors are spring-loaded to ease the force used for repetitive cutting action. (fiskars.com)

8. QUICKUTZ

To operate this personal die-cutting system, place the tool into the desk cradle and use body weight to precision-cut letters and shapes. (quickutz.com)

CROP ON-THE-GO

Tips for Staying Organized

Whether cropping alone or with friends, the enjoyment of your day can be over-shadowed a bit when you are left with a huge mess of paper scraps to clean up and tons of tools to put back in their places. Keep the following tips in mind to make tidying up faster and easier.

CLEAR YOUR DESK

Before you start any scrapbooking session, make sure that your work surface is clutter-free.

TAKE OUT ONLY WHAT YOU NEED

Leave all unneeded tools and supplies tucked away so you have room to spread out. If you are working on a birthday page, place only your balloon print paper and cake die cuts in front of you. If you are working on punch art, take out your punches and cardstock.

CLEAN AS YOU GO

Keep a trash can next to your desk or tape a paper bag to the side of your table. As you crop photos or trim paper accents, be sure to deposit the scraps in the trash as you work. Upon finishing with a tool, put it back in its place. As you complete individual pages, place them in page protectors and file them away.

WRAP UP WITH A CLEAN SWEEP

When finished scrapbooking, clear off any remaining paper scraps, wipe down your work surface, vacuum if necessary and take out the garbage. The next time you are ready to crop, your area will be ready to go.

After you are done scrapbooking, clear off any random items, refile usable paper scraps, wipe down your work surface, vacuum up paper scraps from the floor and take out the garbage. Your area will be ready to go for the next time you crop.

Supply Review and Rotation

As your scrapbooking style evolves, so too will your supply needs. Tools that were once essential may become obsolete. And items you once thought you'd never use may become staples. Periodically review and rotate your supplies to ensure maximum potential.

FOR EVERYTHING, THERE IS A SEASON

Think of your supplies as your scrapbooking wardrobe. Change them with the seasons depending on what projects you are working on. If you are working on a baby album one winter, keep your baby supplies close at hand. Pack away "out-of-season" items—ones you won't be using for several months—until you are ready to start a new project. Like heavy sweaters in the summertime, you won't miss items that you aren't currently using and you'll have more space for the supplies you do need at the time.

SWAP WITH YOURSELF

If you have participated in a swap, you know the excitement of receiving a package filled with brand-new goodies. Experience that same excitement on your own. Instead of keeping all your embellishments close at hand, box some of them up and place them in a closet. Every few months, "swap" with yourself by taking some new items out of the box and putting others away.

WHEN IN DOUBT, DO WITHOUT

Don't hold onto supplies that you aren't using. If something has been in storage for more than a year and you haven't wanted or needed it, then sell it, trade it or give it away.

IN WITH THE NEW, OUT WITH THE OLD

If your scrapbook supply inventory is so large that you can't remember what you have, select an item to give away each time you purchase a new one of a similar type. Don't get rid of necessities such as adhesives, but if a new style of letter stickers catches your eye, search your supplies for a style that is somewhat outdated. Give the outdated style to your kids or donate it to a school or day care.

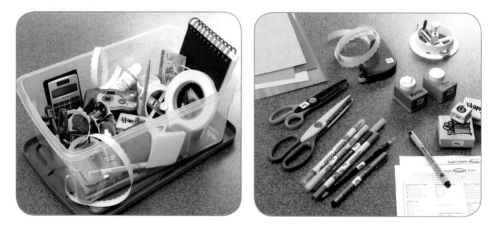

Empty storage areas, bins and drawers of scrapbook supplies and sort and group like items; determine what to get rid of.

CROP ON-THE-GO

What to Do With Unwanted Supplies

Use these ideas to find homes for items that are taking up space and not getting used in your workspace.

DONATE THEM

Give your tools and supplies to a charitable organization, such as a school, church group, baby-sitting co-op, the Picture Me Foundation, Girl or Boy Scouts of America, a nursing home or a children's hospital.

SWAP THEM

Set unwanted items aside for a future in-home or Internet swap (see pp. 216-217).

SELL THEM

Sell the items at a garage sale or the flea market. List items in a local newspaper ad or sell them on an Internet auction. For a minimal fee, some local scrapbook stores may allow you to display your wares on select days. Ask a store owner near you about his or her policy.

REGIFT THEM

Give the items to your children to let them experiment and help them foster a love for preserving memories. If you have quality items that you know will be useful to someone else, wrap the items up for scrapbooking friends.

DISCARD THEM

If the items are simply beyond repair or outdated to the point that your friends wouldn't make good use of them, toss them out for good.

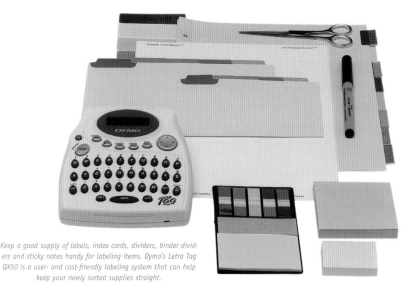

Keep a good supply of labels, index cards, dividers, binder dividers and sticky notes handy for labeling items. Dymo's Letra Tag QX50 is a user- and cost-friendly labeling system that can help keep your newly sorted supplies straight.

CROP ON-THE-GO

How to Host a Swap

One person's trash really is another person's treasure. Swapping an unwanted item for one you will use can help you recoup some of the original cost. You might also be able to sell an item at the swap if you can't find anything to trade. Don't bring home any swapped items that you won't use. To host a successful swap at your home, consider the following tips.

In-Home Swaps

- *Send out invitations at least two to three weeks in advance. Consider making your own from scrapbook supplies to inspire others. Include time, location, RSVP information and what to bring. If you'd like participants to package items for swapping in a certain way, include specifics on the invitation.*

- *Consider making it a themed swap. Try swapping bags of patterned paper, page kits, hand-made cards, birthday theme items or any other topic that is popular among your friends.*

- *Provide large tables for displaying swapped supplies in a room with plenty of open space and comfortable seating.*

- *Make the atmosphere festive with table decorations and music. If hosting a themed swap, decorate to fit the theme. Offer easy-to-eat appetizers and treats so your guests can snack while they swap.*

- *Provide pens, price tags and tally sheets for guests to keep track of trades or purchases.*

- *If you'd like cropping time to following swapping, include this in the invitation so guests will know to bring their supplies.*

Internet Swaps

Swaps on a wide variety of topics are extremely popular on the Internet. Consider joining an online group and become part of the fun yourself.

- *Check out Internet Web sites for more information on swaps: www.scrapbook.com, www.twopeasinabucket.com, www.suite101.com/welcome.cfm/scrapbooking, www. groups.yahoo.com or do a search for "scrapbook swaps."*

- *Determine the style of the swap. For example, try a round-robin swap in which each participant sends a chosen item to the host of the swap in a quantity that will provide each member of the group with one. The host then redistributes the items so that each participant receives a package containing items provided by each member.*

- *Select the type of items to be swapped such as metallics, fibers, letter stickers, etc.*

- *E-mail information regarding your swap to your online buddies or post on a message board.*

- *Provide a complete set of rules to all swappers.*

- *Remind participants to include correct postage on their swap parcels or shipping boxes.*

- *E-mail sender a notice of confirmation upon receipt.*

- *Regularly post the status of the swap on the appropriate Internet message board.*

- *Be punctual in sending swapped materials to participants.*

Starting a Crop Group

Half the fun of being a scrapbooker is socializing with other like-minded enthusiasts. True camaraderie results when you share stories of family and friends and laugh until the wee morning hours, all while preserving cherished memories. But many scrapbookers simply don't schedule enough time for these enjoyable cropping interludes. The solution? Start a crop group to scrapbook with regularly. Getting started is easy with the tips and ideas detailed in the next few pages.

Every year our scrapbook club celebrates National Scrapbook Day. This year our theme was LUAU! Some of us got dressed up and learned a fun dance taught to us by Vanessa. We performed to the song, "Tiny Bubbles". Our event was a blast!

Aloha
DOCUMENT YOUR CROP GROUP

Suzy created this page about the Bay Area Scrappers' annual tradition of celebrating National Scrapbook Day. The group meets in Suzy's garage.

Suzy West, Fremont, California

Supplies: *Patterned papers (SEI); acrylic flower charms (KI Memories); letter stamps (Making Memories); cardstock; ribbon; silk flowers; brads; acrylic paint; stamping ink; hole punch*

Who to Invite

ASK FELLOW SCRAPBOOKERS

The easiest way to form a crop group is to begin with an established group of friends who are interested in scrapbooking. Think of those who have expressed interest in meeting more regularly, or who always seem to make time for scrapbooking. Don't think it has to be a large group—some of the most successful and long-term crop groups are comprised of just a few people.

CONVERT OTHERS

If you don't have many scrapbooking friends, you can always "convert" existing friends or acquaintances. Are you part of a moms' group? Did you just move to a new neighborhood? Invite people with whom you already associate to a scrapbook party at your home. Later, ask your guests if they'd be interested in joining a group.

SEARCH ONLINE

Visit Yahoo Groups (www.groups.yahoo.com) or another scrapbooking site with a message board to see if there is an already-formed group you can join, or post information about starting your own.

VISIT YOUR LOCAL STORE

Many scrapbook stores host crops on their premises. Check your local favorites for a great way to meet fellow enthusiasts.

WHERE TO CROP

As the initiator of the group, you may want to offer your own home, or suggest rotating among members' homes each month. Other good cropping locales include community centers or clubhouses in your neighborhood, a country club (if you're a member) or even your local library. Perhaps members might know of places where the group could meet for free, such as a church someone attends or a small business where a member works.

Agenda

The agenda you choose can range from totally casual cropping to one that may include technique workshops or completing theme-specific pages. Many established groups have a routine, such as starting with show-and-tell to display newly completed pages or a potluck dinner. Whether you choose to schedule lots of activities or participate in nothing aside from scrapbooking (and chatting) will ultimately depend on the personalities of the people involved. In the end, do what would be most fun and inspiring for the group as a whole.

Crop Group Activities

POTLUCK

Tasty food can fuel creative ideas. Have each group member bring a dish to share, and don't forget dessert.

FUN AND GAMES

Pool money to buy fun prizes for winners of games, such as Fastest Page Maker or Most Creative Embellishments. At a sleepover party, add to the fun by weighing each cropper's supplies to see who has the most loot—the one with the heaviest load gets a prize. Play a form of bingo where scrapbookers cross off supplies listed on a bingo card as members use them, from eyelets to ink to hinges.

CHALLENGES

At each get-together, pose a new challenge, such as brainstorming creative titles or including a minimum of four photos on a layout.

RETREATS

Many crop groups try to gather once or twice a year for overnight crops at a fellow scrapbooker's house or for an entire weekend at a nearby recreational destination. The events allow for bonding among the participants and interruption-free cropping.

CRITIQUE SESSION

Create a gallery of pages set up for everyone's viewing and give feedback about the layouts.

SPEAKERS AND TEACHERS

Ask scrapbookers with unique styles or techniques to demonstrate their skills to the group.

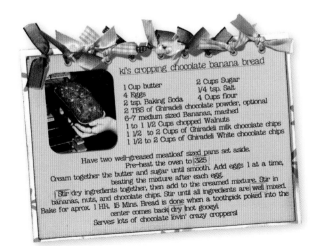

ki's cropping chocolate banana bread

1 Cup butter	2 Cups Sugar
4 Eggs	1/4 tsp. Salt
2 tsp. Baking Soda	4 Cups flour

2 TBS of Ghiradeli chocolate powder, optional
6-7 medium sized Bananas, mashed
1 to 1 1/2 Cups chopped Walnuts
1 1/2 to 2 Cups of Ghiradeli milk chocolate chips
1 1/2 to 2 Cups of Ghiradeli White chocolate chips

Have two well-greased meatloaf sized pans set aside.
Pre-heat the oven to 325
Cream together the butter and sugar until smooth. Add eggs 1 at a time, beating the mixture after each egg.
Stir dry ingredients together, then add to the creamed mixture. Stir in bananas, nuts, and chocolate chips. Stir until all ingredients are well mixed.
Bake for aprox. 1 HR. 15 Mins. Bread is done when a toothpick poked into the center comes back dry not gooey!
Serves lots of chocolate lovin' crazy croppers!

Besides cropping, eating is often a favorite crop group activity. Chocolate is usually a key ingredient. Suzy West, founder of the Bay Area Scrappers, shares a recipe for Cropping Chocolate Banana Bread.

Supplies: *Patterned papers (SEI); green paper (Bazzill); ribbons; eyelets; brown stamping ink; page pebbles; corner rounder punch*

CROP ON-THE-GO

Making the Most of Your Crop Group

MAKE A COMMITMENT

Plan to meet on a regular basis, either weekly, semi-monthly or monthly. While there will always be reasons to not attend, do your best to stay committed to the group in order to keep it going strong.

COME PREPARED

If crop-group night is the only time you have for your hobby, then make the most of it. Bring along only the photos and materials you want to crop so you can sit down and get to work. Consider packing page kits with everything you need for a certain layout in one pack so you don't have to think about where to start.

WORK ON OTHER PROJECTS

When you don't feel like scrapbooking on crop group nights, make tags, cards, sort photos or write journaling notes so you'll be ready to work next time.

PITCH IN FOR COMMUNITY PROPERTY

If all group members use certain larger supplies such as die-cut machines or adhesive application machines, pool money from all members to purchase them. That way, everyone can use the tool and cost is reduced for everyone.

3-D PHOTOS

Using foam spacers between layers of photos to add depth and dimension and to create 3-D photo art.

ABSTRACT SHAPES

Simplified versions of natural shapes, such as symbols denoting restrooms.

ACHROMATIC COLORS

A colorless scheme comprised of blacks, whites and grays.

ACID-FREE

In chemistry, materials that have a pH of 7.0 are neutral. Although acids were once prevalent in photo album papers and products, the damage caused by acids to photographs and memorabilia has been realized and should be avoided. Look for scrapbook products—particularly papers, adhesives and inks—that are free from destructive acids that can eat away at the emulsion on your photos. Harmful acids can occur in the manufacturing process. Check labels for "acid-free" and "photo-safe."

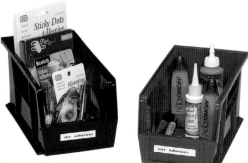

ADHESIVES

A far departure from the gloppy glues of the past, modern adhesives come in both "wet" and "dry" applications depending on one's needs and are used to adhere to photos, accessories and memorabilia to scrapbook pages. Buy and use only acid-free and photo-safe adhesives.

ALBUM

The archival-quality book in which you place your finished scrapbook pages for posterity and for safekeeping. Available in a number of shapes and sizes, albums secure pages in post-bound, binder, spiral or strap-hinge style. Archival albums should be purchased in place of the previously popular magnetic albums, which can destroy photos and memorabilia.

ANALOGOUS COLORS

Colors located next to each other on the color wheel.

ARCHIVAL-QUALITY

Nontechnical term that suggests a material or product is permanent, durable or chemically stable, and that it can be used safely for preservation purposes.

ASYMMETRY

Method of creating balance in which different objects with equal weight are distributed on a page.

BORDER

The upper, lower and side edges or margins of a scrapbook page. Sometimes refers to a border design that is handmade or manufactured and attached to a page.

BUFFERED/ALKALINE RESERVE

Buffering prevents the formation of acids within paper and protects it from exposure to secondary acids from memorabilia, other paper, glues, the atmosphere and oil from fingertips.

BUFFERED PAPER

Paper in which certain alkaline substances have been added during the manufacturing process to prevent acids from forming in the future due to chemical reactions.

CARDSTOCK

The heaviest of scrapbook papers; can be solid colored or patterned. While also used for die cuts and pocket pages, many scrapbookers now look to the innumerable colors of cardstock to serve as page backgrounds.

BALANCE

Equal distribution of weight on a page to create a pleasing arrangement of elements.

BLEEDING

Method of manipulating space in which elements extend over page edges.

CD-ROM

A compact disc that can store large amounts of digitized photos and data files. In scrapbooking, font and lettering CDs as well as scrapbook software CDs have become helpful tools in individually personalizing the page-making process.

COLLAGE

Collage is a collection of different elements adhered together on a page and usually includes photos, embellishments or craft supplies. The elements may or may not overlap.

COLORANTS

Colorants include a wide array of pens, markers, ink pads, chalks, paints and pigment powders—each with its own distinct characteristics and unique properties—made specifically for scrapbooking.

CONCEPT

A central idea or overall theme for a scrapbook page.

CONTRAST

Variations and differences between light and dark colors.

CROP

A term utilized by enthusiasts to describe an event attended by scrapbookers for the purpose of scrapbooking, sharing ideas and tools and swapping products; held at conventions, craft and scrapbook stores, private homes, organized craft events and crop-oriented vacations.

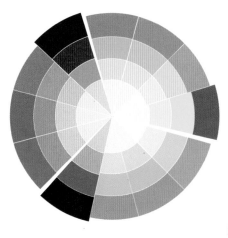

COLOR WHEEL

Artist's tool for matching and coordinating colors, arranged in a circular fashion.

COMPLEMENTARY COLORS

Colors located directly across from one another on the color wheel.

CROPPING

The act of cutting or trimming photos to enhance the image, eliminate unnecessary backgrounds or turn the photos into unique works of art. Early albums most typically displayed photos in their entirety; safe and easy cropping tools have effectively undermined the notion that photographs should not be altered by means of cutting.

send for your FREE TRIAL ISSUE today!

discover page after page of fun designs created by scrappers just like you!

You'll find over 100 innovative ideas in each issue, complete with supplies lists and easy-to-follow instructions. Plus you'll discover the latest tips and techniques you need to preserve your precious memories for generations to come.

☑ **yes!** I'd like to try *Memory Makers* absolutely FREE! Send my complimentary issue and start my trial subscription. If I'm not satisfied, I'll return your invoice marked "cancel" and owe nothing…or I'll honor it and pay just $19.96 plus $3.00 postage and handling for the next eight issues (9 in all). I save 61% off the newsstand price of $59.55!

Name_____

Address _____

City_____State_____ZIP _____

E-mail _____

□ You may contact me about my subscription via e-mail.   J5KUGS
(We won't use your e-mail address for any other purpose.)

send no money now…we'll bill you later!

RUSH!
FREE ISSUE REQUEST!

BUSINESS REPLY MAIL
FIRST-CLASS MAIL   PERMIT NO. 347   FLAGLER BEACH FL

POSTAGE WILL BE PAID BY ADDRESSEE

MEMORY
MAKERS

PO BOX 421400
PALM COAST FL   32142-7160

DE-ACIDIFICATION

To chemically treat paper or memorabilia with a solution that neutralizes acids and builds up an alkaline reserve, which helps prevent future acid migration from damaging photos.

DECORATIVE SCISSORS

While pinking shears were once a fancy departure from traditional straight-edge cutting, there now exists a multitude of scissors with special-cut blades or teeth that provide a wide array of cut patterns, designs and cutting depths. Flipping decorative scissors over will result in a varied cutting pattern.

DIE CUTS

Precut for purchase or self-cut paper shapes that come in both printed and solid colors. Decorative elements for adding a theme or accent to a page. Should be acid- and lignin-free.

DIGITAL

A computer-related term for the process of using numerical digits to create uniform photographic images as shot with a digital camera or scanned into a computer with a scanner.

DIRECTION

The logical path that your eyes should follow through a design.

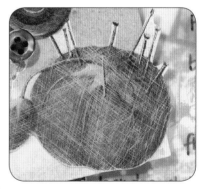

DISTRESS

A creative technique, such as sanding, used to "age" photos, papers and page accents.

DOUBLE COMPLEMENTS

Pairs of complementary colors used together.

DURABILITY

An item's ability to resist the effects of wear and tear from use.

EMBOSS

One of several creative techniques—including wet, dry and heat embossing—used to impress an image or raise an image in a relief.

EMPHASIS

The idea of making a certain element of a design stand out.

ENCAPSULATE

To encase paper or three-dimensional memorabilia in PVC-free plastic sleeves, envelopes and keepers for its own preservation and the protection of your photos.

FIBER-BASED PAPER (FB)

A photographic paper used to develop black-and-white photographs. Because of the way it is made, fiber-based paper can have a 200-year life expectancy (if taken care of and processed correctly). Formerly, it was the standard type of photographic paper, but today fiber-based paper is mainly used for fine-art black-and-white prints.

EMBELLISHMENTS

Page accents that you make or buy. Includes stickers, die cuts, stamped images and punch art. May also include baubles (beads, buttons, rhinestones, sequins), colorants (pens, chalk, inkpads), metallics (charms, wire, jewelry-making components, eyelets, fasteners), textiles (ribbon, embroidery floss, thread) or organics (raffia, pressed flowers and leaves, tiny shells, sand). While one-dimensional accessories traditionally adorned scrapbook pages, there now exists a limitless array of cutting-edge and even three-dimensional products that may be safely used on scrapbook pages.

FOCAL POINT

The central place in which one's attention is drawn in a photo or on a layout.

FONT

A font is a complete set of characters in a particular size and style of type. This includes the letter set, the number set and all of the special character and diacritical marks you get by pressing the shift, option or command/control keys.

FRAMES

Cropping frames for photos is an easy way to add class to your photos without taking attention away from the photo's subject.

GEOMETRIC SHAPES

Structured shapes such as circle, square, rectangle, triangle, etc.

GRID

The structured, underlying framework of a design.

HIERARCHY

A system of organizing information in a design so that the most important elements are emphasized and noticed first.

HUE

The particular shade, lightness or darkness of a color.

ILLUSIONS

Creating photo illusions through creative photo cropping extends the imagery of a conventional photograph. The trickery of photo illusions can exaggerate size and scale, pair unlikely photo subjects for interesting, comical effects or play upon dimension and light.

INITIAL CAP

The first letter of a title or paragraph, designed differently so that it stands out from other elements.

INTENSITY

The strength of a color as related to the purity of that color.

INTERLOCKING

Cropping technique used to tuck slices of papers, photos or page accents into themselves or to join different papers, photos or page accents together.

JOURNALING

Handwritten, handmade or computer-generated text that provides pertinent details about what is taking place in the photographs.

KEY COLOR

Dominant color in a color scheme.

LAYOUT

The final arrangement of paper, title, photos, journaling and page accents on a scrapbook page.

LETTERS, NUMBERS & SYMBOLS

Another fun variation of shape cropping is cutting your photos into letters, numbers and widely recognized symbols. Many templates are available for this use.

LIGHTFASTNESS

A color which is resistant to the action of external agents, such as light, acids, alkalis.

LIGNIN

An organic substance (sap) which acts as a binder for the cellulose fibers in woods and certain plants. It is undesirable in the production of fine papers as it reacts with light/heat to produce phenol (alcohol) and acids which cause deterioration and embrittlement of paper.

LIGNIN-FREE

Paper products that are void of the material (sap) that holds wood fibers together as a tree grows. Most paper is lignin-free except for newsprint, which yellows and becomes brittle with age.

MATTING

The act of attaching paper, generally cropped in the shape of a photo, behind the photo to separate it from the scrapbook page's background paper.

MEMORABILIA

Mementos and souvenirs saved from travel, school and life's special events—things that are worthy of remembrance.

MONOCHROMATIC COLOR

Various shades, hues, tints or tones of one color.

MOOD

The feeling created by choosing certain elements and colors to form a layout or design.

MOSAICS

Pieced photo mosaics are a captivating way to display photos, whether you are cropping and reassembling a single photo or combining several photos.

MOUNTING

Process of attaching photos or memorabilia to an album page. Permanent mounting requires the application of adhesive to the back of a photo or mat. Nonpermanent mounting allows you to attach your items to a page and still have the option of easily removing them.

NATURAL SHAPES

Figures occurring naturally such as the human body, plant and animal shapes.

NEUTRAL COLORS

Black, white, gray, brown and tan.

NON-BLEEDING

A term that describes an ink that does not spread from the original mark on the paper's surface. Non-bleeding depends on both the degree of sizing in the paper and the use of solvents (other than water) in ink.

NON-PERMANENT MOUNTING

Using photo frames, photo corners or pocket sleeves to hold pictures and memorabilia on a page without permanently adhering them.

OPTICAL WEIGHT

The appearance of heaviness or lightness and balance in design, determined by positioning of elements.

ORGANIZATION

The act of putting together photos and memorabilia for the purpose of scrapbooking. Organization of the scrapbook tools and supplies provides for maximum scrapbooking efficiency.

PAGE PROTECTORS

Plastic sleeves or pockets that encase finished scrapbook pages for protection. Use only PVC-free protectors.

PAGE TITLE

A general or descriptive heading put on a scrapbook page that sums up the theme or essence. Conversely, a "title page" is the first at the front of a scrapbook, often decorated and embellished (without photos), that describes the book's content.

PERMANENCE

Ability of a material to resist chemical deterioration, but not a quantifiable term. Permanent paper usually refers to a durable alkaline paper that is manufactured according to ANSI/NISO standards.

PH

The symbol for the degree of acidity or alkalinity of a substance. A pH value of 7.0 is neutral. Less than 7.0 is acidic, more than 7.0 is alkaline.

PHOTOGRAPHIC ACTIVITY TEST (PAT)

A series of tests designed to identify reactivity of photographic images to various elements.

Sometimes we stop on the stairs to *enjoy life*

PHOTOMONTAGE

Montage is similar to collage, but the pictures or parts of pictures are superimposed or overlapped so that they form a blended whole. Photomontages are made strictly of photos, with no other scrapbook embellishments.

PHOTO-SAFE

A term used by companies to indicate that they feel their products are safe to use with photos in a scrapbook album.

PIGMENT INK

Water-insoluble colorants suspended in a liquid—either water, oils or other carriers. Pigments do not penetrate the surface being colored. Instead they adhere to it, providing better contrast and sharpness. For journaling pens and inkpads, look for "acid-free" and "photo-safe" on the label.

PRIMARY COLORS

Red, yellow and blue; no other colors can be mixed together to create these colors.

PROPORTION

The comparative relationship between elements of a design with respect to size, amount and degree.

PUNCHES

Tools in which paper is inserted and pressure is applied to produce particular shapes through a bladed configuration.

RECYCLED PAPER

Paper that meets minimum reclaimed-content standards established by federal, state and municipal governments, and the paper industry. Fiber content usually consists of post- and pre-consumer reclaimed fiber plus virgin pulp.

POCKET PAGE

A scrapbook page that includes some form of a "pocket" in which to place memorabilia or journaling.

REPETITION

Including the same or similar elements more than once in a layout to create rhythm.

POLYETHYLENE (PE)

A polyolefin made from propylene gas. Polypropylene, when free of coatings and additives, is chemically stable. (Used in reference to page protectors.)

RESIN-COATED PAPER (RC)

A photographic paper with a water-resistant backing that absorbs less moisture than fiber-based photos, consequently reducing processing time.

POLYVINYL CHLORIDE (PVC)

A plastic that should not be used in a scrapbook because it emits gases, which cause damage to photos. Use only PVC-free plastic protectors and memorabilia. Safe plastics include polypropylene, polyethylene, and polyester or Mylar.

REVERSE-IMAGE

Reverse-image photos are useful when a mirrored photo effect is desired.

PRESERVATION

The act of stabilizing an item from deterioration through the use of proper methods and materials that maintain the conditions and longevity of the item.

RHYTHM

Rhythm is a term most commonly associated in scrapbooking with creating visual rhythm within design. Rhythm results from a pattern with both repetition and variation of shape, size, color, line, texture or other details. It creates the illusion of movement or motion, which in turn adds energy and excitement to your scrapbook pages.

RULE OF THIRDS

Concept that divides a space into nine equal sections with vertical and horizontal lines; for a pleasing composition, your subject should fall on or near any of the points where the lines intersect.

SANS SERIF

A type style without finishing lines on the ends of letters.

SECONDARY COLORS

Purple, green and orange; colors derived by combining primary colors (red + blue = purple, yellow + blue = green, yellow + red = orange).

SEPIA

A photograph printed in monochromatic brown tints.

SERIF

A type style with tiny lines that finish off the ends of each letter.

SHADE

The degree to which a color is mixed with black.

SHAPE CUTTERS

Bladed tools that are useful for cropping photos, mats and journaling blocks into perfect shapes. They can cut in circles, ovals and many other simple shapes.

SHAPES

Whether freehand cut or cropped with the use of a template, shape cropping adds simple style to scrapbook theme pages while narrowing the focus of the photo's subject.

SILHOUETTE

To trim around the contours of the figures in your photos.

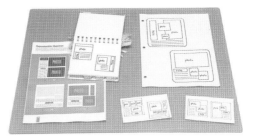

SKETCH

A sketch is a hand-drawn or computer-created blueprint or drawing that shows the approximate placement of a title, journaling and photographs on a layout.

SLICING

Slicing usually involves cropping a photo into slices or segments either freehand or using a craft knife and metal straightedge ruler. Slicing can be horizontal, vertical, straight, wavy or random.

SLIPCASE

An open-ended box that holds a binder. It serves to put contents in dark storage and protect them from dust and light.

SPACE

The distance or area between or around page elements.

TEXT PAPER

A general term for lightweight papers—commonly used for stationery. Text paper is an uncoated printing paper of unusually high quality, available in a wide range of finishes and colors.

TEXTURE

A creative technique, such as crumpling, used to add coarseness or bulk to flat papers.

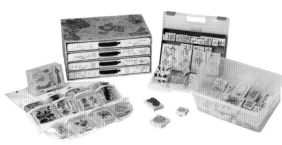

STAMPS

A wood, rubber or clear acrylic tool used to impress a design on paper or cloth; used with a stamp pad or inkpad.

STICKERS

Gummed with adhesive on one side and a design or pattern on the other, stickers are one of the easiest ways to embellish scrapbook pages.

TEARING

Tearing is a great way to add drama or soften photos or papers. Remove the clear plastic backing from a photo to make tearing easier and note the grain on some papers, which are easier to tear in one direction than another. Tear slowly to stay in control of the tear's direction.

TEMPLATES

Templates are stencil-like patterns made of plastic, metal, sturdy paper or cardboard.

VINYL

See polyvinyl chloride.

WEAVING

Cropping and weaving two copies of the same photo together, one in color and one in black-and-white, is a unique and highly visual technique that works great with any photo subject and any photo size. Strips of papers can also be woven together.

Sources

The following companies manufacture products featured in this book. Please check your local retailers to find these materials, or go to a company's Web site for the latest product. In addition, we have made every attempt to properly credit the items mentioned in this book. We apologize to any company that we have listed incorrectly, and we would appreciate hearing from you.

7 Gypsies
(800) 588-6707
www.7gypsies.com

ACD Systems
(250) 544-6700
www.acdsystems.com

Accu-Cut®
(800) 288-1670
www.accucut.com

Adobe Systems Incorporated
(866) 766-2256
www.adobe.com

Advantus Corp.
(904) 482-0091
www.advantus.com

Akro-Mils®
(330) 761-6340
www.akro-mils.com

Alien Skin Software, LLC
(888) 921-SKIN
www.alienskin.com

All Night Media
(see Plaid Enterprises)

American Crafts
(801) 226-0747
www.americancrafts.com

Anna Griffin, Inc.
(888) 817-8170
www.annagriffin.com

ArcSoft®, Inc.
(510) 440-9901
www.arcsoft.com

Armada Art, Inc.
(800) 435-0601
www.armadaart.com

Art Accents, Inc.
www.artaccents.net

ArtBin (a division of Flambeau, Inc.)
(800) 457-5252
www.flambeau.com

ARTchix Studio
(250) 370-9985
www.artchixstudio.com

Bazzill Basics Paper
(480) 558-8557
www.bazzillbasics.com

Bernat®
www.bernat.com

Berwick Offray, LLC
(800) 344-5533
www.offray.com

Big Time Products, LLC (formerly un-du)
(888) Buy-undu
www.un-du.com

Board Dudes, Inc.
(800) 521-4332
www.boarddudes.com

Bo-Bunny Press
(801) 771-4010
www.bobunny.com

Boutique Trims, Inc.
(248) 437-2017
www.boutiquetrims.com

Boxer Scrapbook Productions
(503) 625-0455
www.boxerscrapbooks.com

Broderbund Software
(319) 247-3325
www.broderbund.com

Bunch Of Fun
(877) 419-8488
www.bunchoffun.com

Canon U.S.A., Inc.
(516) 328-5000
www.canon.com

Canson®, Inc.
(800) 628-9283
www.canson-us.com

Caren's Crafts
(805) 520-9635
www.scrapbooking4fun.com

CARL Mfg. USA, Inc.
(800) 257-4771
www.Carl-Products.com

Carolee's Creations®
(435) 563-1100
www.ccpaper.com

Chatterbox, Inc.
(208) 939-9133
www.chatterboxinc.com

Clearsnap, Inc.
(360) 293-6634
www.clearsnap.com

Club Scrap™, Inc.
(888) 634-9100
www.clubscrap.com

Collected Memories
(858) 483-9391
www.collectedmemories.com

Colorbök™, Inc.
(800) 366-4660
www.colorbok.com

Color Wheel Company™, The
(541) 929-7526
www.colorwheelco.com

Concord Camera Corp.
(954) 331-4200
www.concord-camera.com

Corel Corporation
(800) 772-6735
www.corel.com

CottageArts.net™
www.cottagearts.net

Craf-T Products
(507) 235-3996
www.craf-tproducts.com

Creative Imaginations
(800) 942-6487
www.cigift.com

Creative Impressions Rubber Stamps, Inc.
(719) 596-4860
www.creativeimpressions.com

Creative Memories®
(800) 468-9335
www.creativememories.com

Creative Paperclay Company®
(805) 484-6648
www.paperclay.com

Creek Bank Creations, Inc.
(217) 427-5980
www.creekbankcreations.com

Crop In Style®
(888) 700-2202
www.cropinstyle.com

Cropper Hopper™/Advantus Corporation
(800) 826-8806
www.cropperhopper.com

C-Thru® Ruler Company, The
(800) 243-8419
www.cthruruler.com

Cut-It-Up™
(530) 389-2233
www.cut-it-up.com

Daisy D's Paper Company
(888) 601-8955
www.daisydspaper.com

Darice, Inc.
(800_ 321-1494
www.darice.com

Daylight Company, LLC
(866) DAYLIGHT
www.daylightcompany.com

Delta Technical Coatings, Inc.
(800) 423-4135
www.deltacrafts.com

Deluxe Designs
(480) 497-9005
www.deluxedesigns.com

Designer's Library by Lana, The
(660) 582-6484
www.thedesignerslibrary.com

Design Originals
(800) 877-0067
www.d-originals.com

DieCuts with a View™
(877) 221-6107
www.dcwv.com

Display Dynamics, Inc.
(732) 356-1961
www.displaydynamics.net

DMC Corp.
(973) 589-0606
www.dmc.com

DMD Industries, Inc.
(800) 805-9890
www.dmdind.com

Doodlebug Design™ Inc.
(801) 966-9952
www.doodlebug.ws

Duracell
www.duracell.com

Dymo
www.dymo.com

Eagle Affiliates
(800) 643-6798
www.eagleaffiliates.com

Eastman Kodak Company
(770) 522-2542
www.kodak.com

EK Success™, Ltd.
(800) 524-1349
www.eksuccess.com

Energizer Holdings, Inc.
(800) 383-7323
www.energizer.com

Epson America, Inc.
(562) 981-3840
www.epson.com

Ergonomic Services, Inc.
(303) 904-8333
www.ergoservices.net

Family Treasures, Inc.®
www.familytreasures.com

Far and Away
(509) 340-0124
www.farandawayscrapbooks.com

Fellowes, Inc.
(800) 955-0959
www.fellowes.com

Fibers by the Yard™
(405) 364-8066
www.fibersbytheyard.com

Fiskars®, Inc.
(800) 950-0203
www.fiskars.com

Flaming Pear
www.flamingpear.com

FoofaLa
(402) 330-3208
www.foofala.com

Frances Meyer, Inc.®
(413) 584-5446
www.francesmeyer.com

Fuji Photo Film U.S.A., Inc.
(800) 755-3854
www.fujifilm.com

Gauchogirl Creative
www.gauchogirl.com

General Box Company, The- no contact info

Generations
(800) 905-1888
www.generationsnow.com

Glue Dots® International
(888) 688-7131
www.gluedots.com

Grafix®
(800) 447-2349
www.grafix.com

Hallmark Cards, Inc.
(800) 425-6275
www.hallmark.com

Hero Arts® Rubber Stamps, Inc.
(800) 822-4376
www.heroarts.com

Hewlett-Packard Company
www.hp.com/go/scrapbooking

Highsmith, Inc.
(800) 554-4661
www.highsmith.com

Hillcreek Designs
(619) 562-5799
www.hillcreekdesigns.com

Hot Off The Press, Inc.
(800) 227-9595
www.paperpizazz.com

Hunt Corporation
(800) 879-4868
www.hunt-corp.com

Ilford Imaging USA, Inc.
(888) 727-4751
www.printasifun.com

Inkadinkado® Rubber Stamps
(800) 888-4652
www.inkadinkado.com

Ink It- no contact info

Inventor's Studio, The
(866) 799-3653
www.inventorsstudio.com

Jasc Software
(800) 622-2793
www.jasc.com

JewelCraft, LLC
(201) 223-0804
www.jewelcraft.biz

Jo-Ann Stores
(888) 739-4120
www.joann.com

JudiKins
(310) 515-1115
www.judikins.com

Junkitz™
(732) 792-1108
www.junkitz.com

K & Company
(888) 244-2083
www.kandcompany.com

Karen Foster Design
(801) 451-9779
www.karenfosterdesign.com

KI Memories
(972) 243-5595
www.kimemories.com

Kokuyo Co., Ltd.
(877) 465-6589
www.kokuyo-usa.com

Kolo® LLC
(888) 636-5656
www.kolo.com

Konica Minolta Photo Imaging U.S.A., Inc.
(800) 285-6422
www.konicaminolta.com

Kopp Design
(801) 489-6011
www.koppdesign.com

Krylon®
(216) 566-200
www.krylon.com

Lasting Impressions for Paper, Inc.
(801) 298-1979
www.lastingimpressions.com

Light Impressions®
(800) 828-6216
www.lightimpressionsdirect.com

Li'l Davis Designs
(949) 838-0344
www.lildavisdesigns.com

Lion Products- no contact info

LuminArte (formerly Angelwing Enterprises)
(866) 229-1544
www.luminarteinc.com

Magenta Rubber Stamps
(800) 565-5254
www.magentastyle.com

Magic Mesh
(651) 345-6374
www.magicmesh.com

Magic Scraps™
(972) 238-1838
www.magicscraps.com

Making Memories
(800) 286-5263
www.makingmemories.com

Manto Fev™
(402) 505-3752
www.mantofev.com

Ma Vinci's Reliquary
http://crafts.dm.net/mall/reliquary/

Maxell Corporation of America
(800) 533-2836
www.maxell.com

May Arts
(800) 442-3950
www.mayarts.com

McGill, Inc.
(800) 982-9884
www.mcgillinc.com

me & my BiG ideas®
(949) 883-2065
www.meandmybigideas.com

Memories Complete™, LLC
(866) 966-6365
www.memoriescomplete.com

Memory Lane- no contact info

Micrografx®
(972) 234-1769
www.micrografx.com

Microsoft Corporation
www.microsoft.com

Microtek
(310) 687-5940
www.microtek.com

Mrs. Grossman's Paper Company
(800) 429-4549
www.mrsgrossmans.com

Mustard Moon™
(408) 299-8542
www.mustardmoon.com

Nikon™
www.nikon.com

Nova Development Corporation
(818) 591-9600
www.novadevelopment.com

Novelcrafts
(541) 582-3208
www.novelcrafts.com

Nunn Design
(360) 379-3557
www.nunndesign.com

Offray- see Berwick Offray, LLC

Olympus® America, Inc.
(800) 645-8160
www.olympusamerica.com

Ott-Lite Technology®
(800) 842-8848
ww.ott-lite.com

Paintier® Products, LLC
(586) 822-7874
www.paintier.com

Pampered Chef, Ltd., The
(800) 266-5562
www.pamperedchef.com

Paper Adventures®
(800) 525-3196
www.paperadventures.com

Paper Company, The/ANW Crestwood
(800) 525-3196
www.anwcrestwood.com

Paper House Productions®
(800) 255-7316
www.paperhouseproductions.com

Paper Illuzionz
(406) 234-8716
www.paperilluzionz.com

Paper Patch®, The
(800) 397-2737
www.paperpatch.com

Papers by Catherine
(713) 723-3334
www.papersbycatherine.com

Pebbles Inc.
(801) 224-1857
www.pebblesinc.com

Pencil Grip Inc., The
(888) PEN-GRIP
www.thepencilgrip.com

Plaid Enterprises, Inc.
(800) 842-4197
www.plaidonline.com

Polaroid Corp.
(781) 386-2000
www.polaroid.com

Pressed Petals
(800) 748-4656
www.pressedpetals.com

Prickley Pear Rubber Stamps
www.prickleypear.com

PrintWorks
(800) 854-6558
www.printworkscollection.com

Provo Craft®
(888) 577-3545
www.provocraft.com

Prym-Dritz Corporation
www.dritz.com

PSX Design™
(800) 782-6748
www.psxdesign.com

Pulsar Paper Products
(877) 861-0031
www.pulsarpaper.com

Punch Bunch, The
(254) 791-4209
www.thepunchbunch.com

Quantum Storage Systems
(800) 685-4665
www.quantumstorage.com

Quest Beads & Cast, Inc.
(212) 354-0979
www.questbeads.com

QuicKutz, Inc.
(801) 765-1144
www.quickutz.com

Ranger Industries, Inc.
(800) 244-2211
www.rangerink.com

Roxio
(905) 482-5200
www.roxio.com

Rubbermaid
(888) 895-2110
www.rubbermaid.com

Rusty Pickle
(801) 746-1045
www.rustypickle.com

Sakura Hobby Craft
(310) 212-7878
www.sakuracraft.com

Sakura of America
(800) 776-6257
www.sakuraofamerica.com

Sandylion Sticker Designs
(800) 387-4215
www.sandylion.com

ScrapArts
(503) 631-4893
www.scraparts.com

ScrapKings- no contact info

ScrapNCube
(800) 216-4992
www.scrapncube.com

Scrapworks, LLC
(801) 363-1010
www.scrapworks.com

SCS USA/Hemline
(800) 547-8025

SEI, Inc.
(800) 333-3279
www.shopsei.com

Sizzix®
(866) 742-4447
www.sizzix.com

Sonburn, Inc.
(800) 527-7505
www.sonburn.com

Stamp Craft- see Plaid Enterprises

Stampington & Company
(877) STAMPER
www.stampington.com

Stampin' Up!®
(800) 782-6787
www.stampinup.com

Stamppadcaddy
www.stamppadcaddy.com

Stamps by Judith
www.stampsbyjudith.com

Sterilite® Corporation
www.sterilite.com

Sticker Studio™
(208) 322-2465
www.stickerstudio.com

Sturdi-Craft, Inc.
(800) 888-3905
www.sturdicraft.com

Sweetwater
(800) 359-3094
www.sweetwaterscrapbook.com

Therm O Web, Inc.
(800) 323-0799
www.thermoweb.com

Tidy Crafts
(800) 245-6752
www.tidycrafts.com

Timeless Touches™/Dove Valley
Productions, LLC
(623) 362-8285
www.timelesstouches.net

Tombow®
(800) 835-3232
www.tombowusa.com

Traffic Works, Inc.
(323) 582-0616
www.trafficworksinc.com

Tsukineko®, Inc.
(800) 769-6633
www.tsukineko.com

Tutto®/Mascot Metropolitan, Inc.
(800) 949-1288
www.tutto.com

TwinRay
(323) 939-9059
www.twinray.com

USArtQuest, Inc.
(517) 522-6225
www.usartquest.com

Verilux, Inc., "The Healthy
Lighting Company"
(888) 544-4861
www.healthylight.com

Vintage Workshop® LLC, The
(913) 341-5559
www.thevintageworkshop.com

Walnut Hollow® Farm, Inc.
(800) 950-5101
www.walnuthollow.com

Westrim® Crafts
(800) 727-2727
www.westrimcrafts.com

Westwater® Enterprises
(800) 257-4064
www.westwat.com

Wordsworth
(719) 282-3495
www.wordsworthstamps.com

Xyron
(800) 793-3523
www.xyron.com

Index

Learn more with these fine titles from Memory Makers Books!

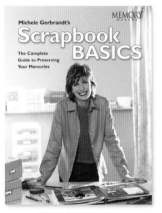

ISBN 1-892127-16-4,
Paperback, 128 pages, #32417

ISBN 1-892127-23-7,
Paperback, 96 pages, #32459

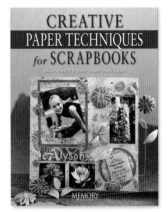

ISBN 1-892127-21-0,
Paperback, 128 pages, #32460

ISBN 1-892127-11-3,
Paperback, 128 pages, #31957

ISBN 1-892127-24-5,
Paperback, 128 pages, #32474

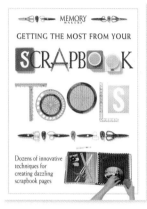

ISBN 1-892127-19-9,
Paperback, 96 pages, #32420

ISBN 1-892127-18-0,
Paperback, 112 pages, #32419

ISBN 1-892127-37-7,
Paperback, 112 pages, #33005

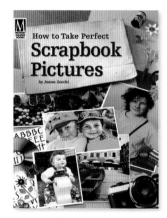

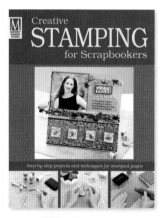

ISBN 1-892127-40-7,
Paperback, 112 pages, #33159

ISBN 1-892127-54-7,
Paperback, 112 pages, #33363

These books and other fine Memory Makers Books titles are available from your local art or
craft retailer, bookstore, on-line supplier or by calling toll free, 1-800-366-6465. Please see page 2
of this book for contact information for Canada, Australia, the U.K. and Europe.